ON THE SUPREME COURT

ON POLITICS
L. Sandy Maisel, Series Editor

On Politics is a series of short reflections by major scholars on key subfields within political science. Books in the series are personal and practical as well as informed by years of scholarship and deliberation. General readers who want a considered overview of a field as well as students who need a launching platform for new research will find these books a good place to start. Designed for personal libraries as well as student backpacks, these smart books are small format, easy reading, aesthetically pleasing, and affordable.

Titles in the Series

LOUIS FISHER

ON THE SUPREME COURT

COURT

Without Illusion and Idolatry

Paradigm Publishers
Boulder • London

Copyright © 2014 by Paradigm Publishers

Published in the United States by Paradigm Publishers, 5589 Arapahoe Avenue, Boulder, CO 80303 USA.

Paradigm Publishers is the trade name of Birkenkamp & Company, LLC, Dean Birkenkamp, President and Publisher.

Library of Congress Cataloging-in-Publication Data

Fisher, Louis.
  On the Supreme Court : without illusion and idolatry / Louis Fisher.
      p. cm. — (On politics)
  Includes bibliographical references and index.
  ISBN 978-1-61205-311-0 (pbk. : alk. paper)
  1. United States. Supreme Court. 2. Judicial process—United States.
3. Judicial review—United States. 4. Civil rights—United States. I. Title.
  KF8742.F5675 2013
  347.73'12—dc23
                                                            2013011436

Printed and bound in the United States of America on acid-free paper that meets the standards of the American National Standard for Permanence of Paper for Printed Library Materials.

18 17 16 15 14   1 2 3 4 5

*It is my pleasure to dedicate this book to
Justice Ruth Bader Ginsburg. I first met her at a conference in
Jerusalem in 1987, where we were invited as speakers. I brought
one of my daughters, Joanna, and she brought her son, James.
They planned a number of tourist outings. At that point Ruth
Ginsburg served on the D.C. Circuit. We remained in touch
after she joined the Supreme Court. President Clinton said that
with her nomination he wanted to hit a home run. In my letter
of congratulation, I told Ginsburg that, as I saw it, the ball left
home plate with a scream, began to rise at second base, and was
still climbing as it left the stadium. Her dedication to public service
continues to reinforce that impression.*

CONTENTS

PREFACE

This book explains how the Supreme Court shares statutory and constitutional interpretation with the elected branches, the fifty states, and the American public. Judicial review does not mean judicial supremacy. Contrary to what is often claimed, the Court's role is not exclusive and detached. It is part of a joint exercise. Over the last five or six decades, however, the Court has been described by scholars and the media as supplying the "final word" on the meaning of the Constitution. Increasingly the Court makes the same claim. It was never the intent of the framers to vest that authority in the Court, it has never functioned in that manner, and it is incompatible with democratic government to assign such overriding political power to the Court.

As with other branches of government, the Supreme Court has had its highs and lows, contributing to individual rights and freedoms in some cases while undermining them in others—strengthening democracy at times, weakening it on other occasions. In its most candid moments, which are, unfortunately, increasingly rare, the Court will look back at a particular decision and publicly admit it was poorly reasoned and damaging to the Court and the nation. All three branches benefit from institutional reflection. The Court is a human institution fully capable of making human mistakes.

We should not study the Supreme Court in isolation.[1] Yet it is now common practice for textbooks on constitutional law to concentrate almost entirely on decisions issued by the Court. The focus is primarily on case law, with little attention to the important contributions by nonjudicial institutions at the national and state levels. The result, as noted by one law professor, is the absence of a "comprehensive course on constitutional law in any meaningful sense in American law schools."[2] Political scientists used to supply a broader, richer, and more realistic view of constitutional interpretation. Over time, they have moved toward the law school model as well.

Those who teach in law schools and political science departments may find it more convenient to study celebrated Court decisions and ignore the contributions of Congress, the president, and the states. That approach, however, poorly serves students, the public, and our constitutional system. It places upon the Court an expectation it cannot meet. Lord Radcliffe advised in a legal essay that "we cannot learn law by learning law." The study of law must be "a part of history, a part of economics and sociology, a part of ethics and

---

1. My textbook American Constitutional Law, coauthored with Katy J. Harriger, combines readings that are both judicial and nonjudicial. Now in its tenth edition (2013), it presents constitutional law as an ongoing dialogue among all three branches at the national level and all fifty states.

2. W. Michael Reisman, "International Incidents: Introduction to a New Genre in the Study of International Law," 10 Yale J. Int'l L. 1, 8 n.13 (1984).

a philosophy of life. It is not strong enough in itself to be a philosophy in itself."[3]

To infuse law with dignity, majesty, and perhaps a touch of mystery, it is customary to make entirely unrealistic claims about the power and authority of the Supreme Court. Those who speak accurately about the Court's role are said to threaten judicial symbols and mythology. Scholars began to draw an arbitrary and imaginary line to separate law from politics. In 1914, when legal philosopher Morris Raphael Cohen began describing how judges made law, his colleagues warned against his research. The deans of major law schools advised that his findings, no matter how solidly based on evidence, might invite even greater recourse to "judicial legislation." Cohen rejected their counsel. He had "an abiding conviction that to recognize the truth and adjust oneself to it is in the end the easiest and more advisable course." He denied that the law is a "closed, independent system having nothing to do with economics, political, social, or philosophical science." If courts were in fact constantly making and remaking the law, it became "of the utmost social importance that the law should be made in accordance with the best available information, which it is the object of science to supply."[4]

In a perceptive essay published in 1969, political scientist C. Herman Pritchett explained that the disciplines of law and political science drifted apart for semantic, philosophical, and practical reasons: "Law is a prestigious symbol, whereas politics tends to be a dirty word. Law is stability; politics is chaos. Law is impersonal; politics is personal. Law is given;

---

3. Lord Radcliffe, The Law & Its Compass 92–93 (1960).

4. Morris R. Cohen, Law and the Social Order 380–81, n.86 (1933).

politics is free choice. Law is reason; politics is prejudice and self-interest. Law is justice; politics is who gets there first with the most."[5] These are stereotypes, of course. At different periods law can be a dirty word, chaotic, personal, a matter of free choice, based on prejudice and self-interest, and a game of who gets there first with the most votes.

Under popular government, the Supreme Court cannot have the last word on constitutional issues. Judicial rulings about speech, press, religious liberty, and other values should not be left to five unelected justices of the Court. Their decisions merit respect, but the finality of Court rulings does not depend on some claim of superior and unchecked power. It depends on the quality of legal (and political) reasoning. Decisions that fail in judgment are necessarily temporary in nature, to be changed by subsequent courts and by other institutions and public pressure. Some may regret that nonjudicial forces compete with, and prevail over, the Court, but this historical pattern is clear and needs to be understood. That is the purpose of this book. In studying the reversals and modifications of Court decisions, we can appreciate how they regularly serve the interests of the nation and its aspiration for democratic rule.

In 2006, Chief Justice John Roberts and Justice Samuel Alito agreed that constitutional interpretation is not a judicial monopoly. Alito said that "all public servants, not just judicial officers, play a role in shaping our law, interpreting our Constitution." It would be a mistake, he said, for "any public officials to ignore questions about the bounds of their

---

5. C. Herman Pritchett, "The Development of Judicial Research," in Joel B. Grossman & Joseph Tanenhaus, eds., Frontiers of Judicial Research 31 (1969).

authority in our constitutional system and simply say that the courts will sort that out for them." Roberts presented a similar theme: "The great gift of the founding generation was the right of self-government. We shouldn't give it up so easily to think that all the important issues are going to be decided by the Supreme Court."[6] Important points, but both Roberts and Alito in the 2010 *Citizens United* decision claimed that the Court could override elected branch policy about campaign expenditures by corporations and unions. (*Citizens United* is explored in Chapter Four.) Two years later, in a case involving the Affordable Care Act, Roberts deferred to policy enacted by Congress and the president. Alito did not.

This preface concludes by comparing two extremes: (1) the claim that the Supreme Court is indeed the final word on the meaning of the Constitution and (2) the counterargument that it is not. Interestingly, both arguments were once made by the same person in the same year: Justice Robert H. Jackson. In a sentence rendered almost hypnotic by its elegant phrasing, he said in 1953: "We are not final because we are infallible, but we are infallible only because we are final."[7] The historical record demonstrates overwhelmingly that the Court is neither infallible nor final. That same year, in an address delivered at a conference, Jackson denied that the judiciary carries out its duties isolated from politics: "Let us not deceive ourselves; long-sustained public opinion does influence the process of constitutional interpretation. Each new member of the ever-changing personnel of our courts brings to his task the assumptions and accustomed thought

---

6. Robert Barnes, "New Justices Take the Podium, Putting Personalities on Display," Washington Post, November 20, 2006, at A15.

7. Brown v. Allen, 344 U.S. 443, 540 (1953).

of a later period. The practical play of the forces of politics is such that judicial power has often delayed but never permanently defeated the persistent will of a substantial majority."[8]

As explained in this book, Jackson considerably understated the interaction between law and politics. Successful challenges to Supreme Court decisions on constitutional issues need not await changes in personnel. The elected branches have the capacity to change constitutional doctrine in the same year that the Court decides a case. Specific examples of this democratic and constructive dialogue are provided.

---

8. Robert H. Jackson, "Maintaining Our Freedoms: The Role of the Judiciary," delivered to the American Bar Association, Boston, Massachusetts, August 24, 1953, reprinted in Vital Speeches, No. 24, Vol. xix, p. 761 (October 1, 1953).

ACKNOWLEDGMENTS

Friends and colleagues gave valuable advice on my basic theme and the cases I selected: Jeff Crouch, Neal Devins, Nancy Kassop, and Mort Rosenberg. Those who read the draft manuscript and helped guide me on many matters of style and substance, including broad patterns: Reb Brownell, Henry Cohen, Chris Edelson, Mike Shenkman, Mitch Sollenberger, and Ilda Yescas. My deep appreciation to all. I am also grateful to the William & Mary Law School for giving me access to their online materials—a very great convenience for someone who retired from the Library of Congress, where I had ready access to whatever I needed. I appreciate the careful and thoughtful copyediting by Candace Cunningham.

CHAPTER ONE
EXERCISING JUDICIAL REVIEW

On what authority does the federal judiciary exercise judicial review: declaring unconstitutional actions by Congress, the president, federal agencies, and the states? The Supreme Court often refers to the U.S. Constitution as one of "enumerated powers," as though each power granted to the national government were expressly stated in the Constitution. In 1995, while striking down a congressional effort to regulate guns in schoolyards, the Court announced: "We start with first principles. The Constitution creates a Federal Government of enumerated powers."[1] Two years later, while invalidating a religious freedom statute, the Court again stated: "Under our Constitution, the Federal Government is one of enumerated powers."[2]

Those statements are highly misleading and erroneous. If the U.S. Constitution were limited to enumerated or express powers, the Court would have no authority to exercise judicial review. Nowhere does the Constitution expressly grant the Court the power of judicial review. It is an *implied* power. The

---

1. United States v. Lopez, 514 U.S. 549, 552 (1995).
2. Boerne v. Flores, 521 U.S. 507, 516 (1997).

president and Congress have a number of implied powers as well, including the president's power to remove department heads and the power of Congress to conduct investigations and hold individuals in contempt. Implied powers must be reasonably drawn from enumerated powers. Article II, Section 3, directs the president to "take Care that the Laws be faithfully executed." If a department head were unwilling or unable to carry out a statutory duty, the president possesses an implied power to remove that person. Article I, Section 1, vests "all legislative Powers herein granted" in a Congress. On what grounds does the Supreme Court have the implied power of judicial review?

Declaring Independence from England

In the years leading up to America's rupture with England in 1776, several famous legal challenges were leveled at the British Parliament. In 1761, James Otis in America argued that British customs officials lacked authority to use general search warrants. Even if the British Parliament had authorized what were called writs of assistance to conduct those searches against American colonists, he said the statute would be "against the Constitution," against "natural equity," and therefore void (see Box 1.1). Five years later, a Virginia court held invalid the Stamp Act, a British statute that attempted to tax every item in America made of paper, including court documents, college diplomas, liquor licenses, newspapers, and playing cards.[3] Colonial resistance to the statute was so fierce

---

3. Edmund S. Morgan & Helen M. Morgan, The Stamp Act Crisis: Prologue to Revolution (1962 ed.).

that England decided to rescind it. On the eve of the Declaration of Independence, a Massachusetts judge instructed the jury to treat acts of Parliament that violated fundamental law as "void" and "inoperative."[4]

The proposition that British courts could void an act of Parliament appeared in an opinion by Chief Justice Edward Coke in 1610. He concluded that when an act of Parliament "is against common right and reason, or repugnant, or impossible to be performed, the common law will controul it, and adjudge such Act to be void."[5] A few British judges in the

---

Box 1.1

James Otis and Fundamental Law

This writ [of assistance] is against the fundamental principles of law. The privilege of the House. A man who is quiet, is as secure in his house, as a prince in his castle—notwithstanding all his debts and civil processes of any kind....

For flagrant crimes and in cases of great public necessity, the privilege may be infringed on. For felonies an officer may break upon process and oath, that is, by a special warrant to search such a house, sworn to be suspected, and good grounds of suspicion appearing....

As to Acts of Parliament. An act against the Constitution is void; an act against natural equity is void; and if an act of Parliament should be made, in the very words of this petition, it would be void. The executive Courts must pass such acts into disuse.

Source: 2 The Works of John Adams 521–22, 523–25 (Charles Francis Adams, ed.).

---

4. Edward S. Corwin, The Doctrine of Judicial Review 32 (1914).

5. Dr. Bonham's Case, 77 Eng. Rep. 646, 652 (1610). Details on this case are provided in Louis Fisher, Defending Congress and the Constitution 24–25 (2011).

seventeenth and eighteenth centuries relied on Coke's decision, but the principle of judicial review never took root on English soil.[6] Although Coke's opinion provided inadequate support for judicial review, it was accepted as good law and precedent for those in America who wanted to break with England. To avoid the appearance of impetuous and impulsive behavior by American colonists, Coke's opinion helped provide intellectual justification for opposing British rule.

From independence to the drafting of the U.S. Constitution, some state judges in America challenged the statutes of their legislatures. Scholars disagree on the legitimacy of those rulings, but decisions offering support for judicial review were handed down by judges in Virginia, New Jersey, New York, Connecticut, Rhode Island, and North Carolina. It is recognized that the apparently powerful language used by judges in holding state laws invalid was often in excess of the results they achieved.[7]

By the time of the Philadelphia Convention in 1787, some of the delegates expected judicial review to be part of the new national government. Their statements were not always clear or consistent. There was general agreement that the Articles of Confederation during the War of Independence had to be replaced by giving stronger powers to a central government. Instead of the legislative supremacy that existed under the Articles of Confederation, Congress would be one of three coordinate branches. Both the Virginia Plan presented by Edmund Randolph and the New Jersey Plan submitted by

---

6. Day v. Savadge, 80 Eng. Rep. 235, 237 (1614); The City of London v. Wood, 88 Eng. Rep. 1592, 1602 (1702).

7. Charles Grove Haines, The American Doctrine of Judicial Supremacy 88–120 (1932).

William Paterson called for the creation of an independent judiciary headed by a Supreme Court.

The framers worried that thirteen sets of state courts would issue inconsistent rulings on matters of national concern. Several essays in the *Federalist Papers,* published in 1788 to promote ratification of the U.S. Constitution, called attention to this problem. In Federalist No. 80, Alexander Hamilton warned that thirteen independent courts of final jurisdiction at the state level "over the same causes, arising upon the same laws, is a hydra in government from which nothing but contradiction and confusion can proceed." The convention responded to that issue by adopting the Supremacy Clause in Article VI of the Constitution: the Constitution and all national laws, including treaties, "shall be the supreme Law of the Land; and the Judges in every State shall be found thereby, any Thing in the Constitution or Laws of any State to the Contrary notwithstanding." Judicial review over presidential and congressional actions, however, posed a subject of much greater delicacy. Giving federal courts the final say over actions by the elected branches was an extreme position.

Scholars have spent much time counting the number of framers who favored judicial review. Over the years, constitutional scholar Edward Corwin vacillated on the statistics, ranging from a high of seventeen framers to a low of five or six.[8] In testifying before Congress in 1937, Corwin uttered this scholar's lament: "These people who say the framers intended [judicial review] are talking nonsense; and the people who say they did not intend it are talking nonsense.

---

8. Leonard D. Levy, ed., Judicial Review and the Supreme Court 3–4 (1967).

There is evidence on both sides."[9] Many studies have been infused with a crusading spirit, designed either to prove the historical legitimacy of judicial review or to chop away at its foundations.[10] The unsettled nature of judicial review—or at least its scope—adds some constraint to judicial activism.

Judicial review was discussed at the Philadelphia Convention as a means of checking Congress and the states. On May 29, Randolph proposed a Council of Revision consisting of "the Executive and a convenient number of the National Judiciary ... with authority to examine every act of the National Legislature before it shall operate, & every act of a particular Legislature before a Negative [presidential veto] thereon shall be fatal; and that the dissent of the said Council shall amount to a rejection, unless the Act of the National Legislature be again passed."[11] The eventual elimination of this council is accepted by some as evidence that the framers rejected judicial review. However, a major argument against the council was the *availability* of judicial review. One of the framers, Elbridge Gerry, expressed "doubts whether the Judiciary ought to form a part of it, as they will have a sufficient check agst. encroachments on their own department by their exposition of the laws, which involve a power of deciding on their Constitutionality." In some states, courts

---

9. Senate Committee on the Judiciary, "Reorganization of the Federal Judiciary" (Part 2), 75th Cong., 1st Sess. 176 (1937).

10. For support of judicial review: Charles A. Beard, The Supreme Court and the Constitution (1912) and Raoul Berger, Congress v. The Supreme Court (1989). Critics include Louis B. Boudin, Government by Judiciary (1932), and William W. Crosskey, Politics and the Constitution (1953).

11. 1 Records of the Federal Convention of 1787, at 21 (Max Farrand, ed., 1966 paperback). Hereafter "Farrand."

had set aside laws "as being agst. the Constitution. This was done too with general approbation."[12]

The delegates debated a congressional veto over state legislation. This power was rejected for two reasons. The addition of the Supremacy Clause would presumably handle any conflicts between national law and state legislation. Moreover, state courts could exercise judicial review to control legislative errors. James Madison said that a law "violating a constitution established by the people themselves, would be considered by the Judges as null & void."[13] Those statements were clearly limited to judicial review at the state—not the national—level.

Ratification Debates

At the ratification conventions in 1788, several delegates defended judicial review. James Wilson, soon to be a member of the Supreme Court, told his colleagues at the Pennsylvania ratification convention that the legislature would be "kept within its prescribed bounds" by the judiciary.[14] At the Connecticut ratifying convention, Oliver Ellsworth (destined to be the third chief justice of the Supreme Court) expected federal judges to void any legislative act that was contrary to the Constitution.[15] At the Virginia ratifying convention, John

---

12. Id. at 97.

13. 2 Farrand 93.

14. 2 Debates in the Several State Conventions, on the Adoption of the Federal Constitution 445 (Jonathan Elliot, ed., 1836–1845). Hereafter "Elliot."

15. Id. at 131.

Marshall anticipated that the federal judiciary would strike down unconstitutional legislative acts.[16] Given the context of these remarks, it appears that the availability of judicial review was used to reassure the states that national power would be held in check.

The *Federalist Papers* include several essays that speak strongly for judicial review. The principal essay, Federalist No. 78, by Hamilton, was designed to allay state fears about national power. He argued that the judiciary was "the least dangerous" of the three branches because it lacked the president's "sword" and Congress's "purse." The judiciary, in his words, "may truly be said to have neither Force nor Will, but merely judgment." The Antifederalists, opposed to the draft constitution, took a more realistic view of judicial power. In the *Anti-Federalist Papers,* Letter XI from "Brutus" worried that judicial review at the national level would weaken the powers of the states, Congress, and the president. Any errors committed in federal courts could not be "corrected by any power above them, if any such power there be." From the decisions of the federal courts there appeared to be "no appeal" other than to the Supreme Court. The impeachment power, Brutus said, would be an unlikely check on judicial power.[17] Some of Hamilton's arguments were later borrowed by John Marshall to buttress his case for judicial review in *Marbury* v. *Madison* (see Box 1.2).

Some meaning about the scope of judicial review comes from debates at the Philadelphia Convention on this language in Article III, Section 2: "The judicial Power shall extend to all Cases, in Law and Equity, arising under this Constitution,

---

16. Id. at 553.

17. Herbert J. Storing, ed., The Anti-Federalist 163–65 (1985 ed.).

> **Box 1.2**
>
> **Hamilton in Federalist No. 78**
>
> There is no position which depends on clearer principles, than that every act of a delegated authority, contrary to the tenor of the commission under which it is exercised, is void. No legislative act, therefore, contrary to the Constitution, can be valid. To deny this, would be to affirm, that the deputy is greater than his principal; that the servant is above his master; that the representatives of the people are superior to the people themselves; that men acting by virtue of powers, may do not only what their powers do not authorize, but what they forbid.

the Laws of the United States, and Treaties made." In most of the early drafts, the language "arising under" applied only to laws passed by Congress. When William Samuel Johnson moved to insert the words "this Constitution" before the text "the Laws," Madison objected, stating that he "doubted whether it was not going too far to extend the jurisdiction of the Court generally to cases arising Under the Constitution, & whether it ought to be limited to cases of a Judiciary Nature. The right of expounding the Constitution in cases of this nature ought not to be given to that Department." Johnson's motion was agreed to without further discussion, "it being generally supposed that the jurisdiction given was constructively limited to cases of a Judiciary nature."[18]

We are left to wonder about the meaning of "a judiciary nature." Evidently this amendment to Article III indicated something less than full-blown judicial review, to be exercised without limits. Certainly judicial review would be appropriate

---

18. 2 Farrand 430.

to protect the independence of the courts, such as in the instance of a bill decreasing judicial salaries, in direct violation of language in Article III, Section 1, that prohibits any diminishment of judicial compensation. It would apply also to congressional actions specifically prohibited by Article I, Section 9, such as passing a bill of attainder (legislative punishment without judicial trial) or an *ex post facto* law. Beyond those categories, the scope of judicial review has been defined by practice, including some judicial self-inflicted injuries covered in Chapters Three, Four, and Five.

Sources of Judicial Authority

Under Article III, Section 1, the "judicial Power of the United States" is vested "in one supreme Court, and in such inferior Courts as the Congress may from time to time ordain and establish." Federal judges "shall hold their Offices during good Behaviour, and shall, at stated Times, receive for their Services, a Compensation, which shall not be diminished during their Continuance in Office." The prohibition on salary reductions helps protect the independence of the judiciary.

Section 2 extended the judicial power to "all Cases, in Law and Equity, arising under this Constitution, the Laws of the United States, and Treaties made, or which shall be made, under their Authority." These cases may affect ambassadors, other public ministers, consuls, admiralty, and maritime jurisdiction. They may also include disputes in which the national government shall be a party and controversies between two or more states, between a state and citizens of another state, between citizens of the same state claiming lands under grants of different states, and between a state "or the Citizens thereof, and foreign States, Citizens or Subjects."

In 1793, the Supreme Court held that a state could be sued in federal court by citizens of another state.[19] This decision prompted a constitutional amendment to change Section 2. The Eleventh Amendment, ratified on February 7, 1795, provides: "The Judicial power of the United States shall not be construed to extend to any suit in law or equity, commenced or prosecuted against one of the United States by Citizens of another State, or by Citizens of any Foreign State." Other Supreme Court cases have been overturned by constitutional amendments. The Fourteenth Amendment nullified the Court's 1857 decision in *Dred Scott* v. *Sandford,* which held that blacks as a class were not citizens protected under the Constitution, and that Congress could not prohibit slavery in the territories.[20] The Sixteenth Amendment overruled the Court's decision in *Pollock* v. *Farmers' Loan and Trust Co.,* which had struck down a federal income tax.[21] The Twenty-sixth Amendment was ratified in 1971 to overturn a Supreme Court decision of the previous year that voided a congressional effort to lower the minimum voting age in state elections to eighteen.[22]

Section 2 explains that the Court has two types of jurisdiction: cases that come initially to the Court (original jurisdiction) and those that come only after lower courts have reached a judgment (appellate jurisdiction). Original jurisdiction applies to all cases "affecting Ambassadors, other public

---

19. Chisholm v. Georgia, 2 Dall. (2 U.S.) 419 (1793).
20. 60 U.S. (19 How.) 393 (1857).
21. 158 U.S. 601 (1895).
22. Oregon v. Mitchell, 400 U.S. 112 (1970).

Ministers, and Consuls, and those in which a State shall be Party." In other cases the Court has appellate jurisdiction, "both as to Law and Fact, with such Exceptions, and under such Regulations as the Congress shall make." That language makes judicial independence subject to congressional controls.

The final part of Section 2 covers trials and impeachment. The trial of all crimes, "except in Cases of Impeachment," shall be by jury, and such trials shall be held in the state where the crime has been committed. When not committed within any state, the trial "shall be at such Place or Places as the Congress may by Law have directed." This is another example of congressional control over the judiciary. Article I, Section 3, explains that when the president is tried before the Senate for impeachment, the chief justice shall preside.

Article III concludes with Section 3, which defines treason as "levying war" against the United States "or adhering to their Enemies, giving them Aid and Comfort." No person shall be convicted of treason unless on the testimony of two witnesses "to the same overt Act, or on Confession in open Court." The Congress shall have power to declare the punishment of treason, but "no Attainder of Treason shall work Corruption of Blood, or Forfeiture except during the Life of the Person attainted." The purpose of this provision is to prohibit holding children accountable for treasonous acts of their parents. Actions by an individual may not legally taint the rest of the family.

Nothing in Article III appears to directly empower the Supreme Court to exercise judicial review. Language in Article VI holds some promise: "This Constitution, and the Laws of the United States which shall be made in Pursuance thereof; and all Treaties made, or which shall be made, under the Authority of the United States, shall be the supreme Law of the Land; and the Judges in every State shall be bound thereby, any Thing in the Constitution or Laws of any State to the Contrary notwithstanding." However, this provision may sanction judicial review over the states, not over Congress and the president.

Steps toward Judicial Review

Marbury v. *Madison,* discussed in the next section, is generally cited as the source of judicial review. In fact, judicial review was recognized much earlier. When Madison introduced the Bill of Rights in the House of Representatives in 1789, he predicted that once those rights were incorporated into the Constitution, "independent tribunals of justice will consider themselves in a peculiar manner the guardians of those rights; they will be an impenetrable bulwark against every assumption of power in the Legislative or Executive."[23] His prediction was quite wide of the mark. Federal courts would not be such reliable guardians of individual rights.

Nine days after speaking about the Bill of Rights, Madison offered his thoughts on whether the president had an implied power to remove certain executive officials. He disagreed that Congress should defer to the judiciary on this constitutional issue. On what principle, he asked, could it be contended "that any one department draws from the Constitution greater powers than another, in marking out the limits of the powers of the several departments?" If questions arose on the boundaries between the branches, he did not see "that any one of these independent departments has more right

---

23. 1 Annals of Cong. 439 (June 8, 1789).

than another to declare their sentiments on that point."[24] Under that interpretation, Madison did not believe that the elected branches should be subordinate to the judiciary on constitutional questions.

In 1792, three federal circuit courts objected to a congressional statute that appointed federal judges to serve as commissioners for settling claims by private individuals. Under the statute, their judgments could be set aside by the Secretary of War. Why should federal judges be placed in a subordinate position: performing nonjudicial duties and then having their conclusions overridden by an executive officer? After these constitutional objections had been raised in very frank fashion, and before the Supreme Court could rule on the issue, Congress repealed the offending sections and removed the Secretary's authority to veto decisions reached by judges.[25] In 1794, after Congress fixed the statute, the Supreme Court observed that the original statute would have been unconstitutional had it been tested in the courts, implying judicial review.[26] This decision, left unpublished until 1851, is not an example of judicial review. The Court referred to a statute that had already been repealed.

From 1789 to 1802, state courts began to exercise judicial review over state statutes. Over that same period, federal courts struck down a number of state laws.[27] Judicial review by the federal judiciary over the states was thus well established. The application of judicial review against the coequal

24. Id. at 500 (June 17, 1789).

25. Hayburn's Case, 2 Dall. 409 (1792); 1 Stat. 243 (1792); 1 Stat. 324 (1793).

26. United States v. Yale Todd, 13 How. 52 (1794).

27. 1 Charles Warren, The Supreme Court in United States History 65–69 (1937).

branches of Congress and the president was a bolder claim to assert. In 1796, the Supreme Court upheld a congressional statute that imposed a tax on carriages.[28] If it possessed authority to sustain a congressional statute, presumably it could strike one down. In any event, the Court had reviewed the constitutionality of the statute and found it permissible. In the carriage case, Justice Samuel Chase said it was unnecessary "*at this time,* for me to determine, whether this court, *constitutionally* possesses the power to declare an act of Congress *void,* on the ground of its being made contrary to, and in violation of, the Constitution; but if the court have such power, I am free to declare, that I will never exercise it, *but in a very clear case.*"[29]

In moving toward judicial review, in the sense of declaring a congressional or presidential act unconstitutional, the Court stepped very cautiously. Two years later, the Court upheld the constitutionality of procedures followed by Congress for constitutional amendments.[30] In other cases between 1798 and the issuance of *Marbury* in 1803, Supreme Court justices continued to tiptoe around the existence of their authority to invalidate congressional statutes.[31]

Although these justices spoke guardedly about the power of judicial review, members of Congress had no hesitation about saying that the power existed and was legitimate. They understood that the Constitution placed limits on the elected branches, and that the courts were available to monitor unconstitutional actions. Representative James Bayard

---

28. Hylton v. United States, 3 Dall. 171 (1796).

29. Id. at 175 (emphases in original).

30. Hollingsworth v. Virginia, 3 Dall. 378 (1798).

31. E.g., see the remarks by Justices Chase and Iredell in Calder v. Bull, 3 Dall. 386, 392, 395, 399 (1798), and by Justice Chase in Cooper v. Telfair, 4 Dall. 14, 19 (1800).

remarked in 1802: "To maintain, therefore, the Constitution, the judges are a check upon the Legislature. The doctrine I know is denied, and it is therefore incumbent upon me to show that it is sound."[32] Like Justice Chase, Bayard supported judicial review only in very clear cases. For example, Article I, Section 9, prohibits Congress from passing a bill of attainder. Article I, Section 10, applies the same prohibition to the states. If Congress or a state were to pass such a bill, Bayard said, the courts "are bound to decide."[33] He offered another example that would warrant judicial review. Article I, Section 9, empowers Congress to suspend the privilege of habeas corpus when in cases of "Rebellion or Invasion the public safety may require it." Bayard asked, "Suppose a law prohibited the issuing of the writ at a moment of profound peace?"[34] To Bayard, judges would be required to take a case challenging the suspension and reach an independent judgment.

Like Madison, Thomas Jefferson hoped that federal courts would consider themselves as guardians of constitutional rights and strike down governmental actions that violated those rights. He wanted courts to invalidate the repressive Alien and Sedition Acts of 1798. He appealed to the courts to protect fundamental rights: "The laws of the land, administered by upright judges, would protect you from any exercise of power unauthorized by the Constitution of the United States."[35] Both men would be disappointed by the performance of federal judges. A Federalist Congress and a Federalist president (John Adams) enacted the Alien

---

32. 11 Annals of Cong. 645 (1802).

33. Id.

34. Id. at 647.

35. 10 Writings of Thomas Jefferson 61 (Albergh Ellery Bergh, ed., 1903).

and Sedition Acts. Federalist judges were not about to rule against them.

Political conditions in the United States changed radically in 1800. After twelve years of Federalist Party control, the Jeffersonians swept the elections, gaining control over both Congress and the White House. The only branch left under Federalist control was the judiciary. In February 1801, with only a few weeks left in the lame-duck Congress, the Federalists passed two bills to fortify their political power. One statute created sixteen lifetime judges to serve in newly created circuits, relieving Supreme Court justices of the need to "ride circuit" over long distances and very unsafe traveling conditions to hear appellate cases.[36] The other statute created new justices of the peace for the District of Columbia, each with a five-year term.[37] President Adams quickly nominated Federalists to these new judicial positions. The Federalist Senate moved with speed to confirm them. One day before Jefferson took the oath of office as president, the Senate confirmed forty-two justices of the peace.[38] This was an early version of court-packing. During the remaining days of the Adams administration, John Marshall served as Secretary of State even though he had already been confirmed for the Supreme Court in the next term. After the Senate confirmed the judicial positions, Marshall was supposed to deliver the commissions to the new office-holders. Because of last-minute pressures and distractions, some were never delivered, including one for William Marbury to be justice of the peace in the District of Columbia.

---

36. 1 Stat. 89 (1801).

37. 1 Stat. 103, 107, sec. 11 (1801).

38. William W. Van Alstyne, "A Critical Guide to Marbury v. Madison," 1969 Duke L. J. 1, 4 (1969).

The Poorly Understood *Marbury* Case

Upon entering the White House, Jefferson ordered the with-holding of judicial nominations confirmed by the Federalist Senate and signed and sealed by President Adams but not yet delivered. He also urged Congress to repeal the Circuit Court Act of 1801 (with its additional sixteen lifetime judges) and to cancel the anticipated 1802 term for the Supreme Court. Congress passed both measures.[39] To their dismay, Supreme Court justices had to return to circuit-riding. Through various actions, the two elected branches were squaring off against the Federalist judiciary. Chief Justice Marshall saw the confrontation and understood the dangers to the judiciary. Far from brashly using judicial review to empower the Court, Marshall had the institutional sense and judgment to avoid a showdown. It is a complicated story, but must be understood to avoid widespread misconceptions about *Marbury*.

The House of Representatives impeached District Judge John Pickering (a Federalist) and the Senate removed him. As a next step, the House impeached Justice Samuel Chase, of course another Federalist. Chief Justice Marshall had every reason to believe he might be the next target. Something he understood with total clarity: any attempt by him to compel President Jefferson or Secretary of State Madison to deliver the commissions to Marbury and the others would be ignored. A collision between the judiciary and the elected branches was coming. How could Marshall minimize the damage to his institution? It was not by beating his breast and claiming judicial supremacy. He knew the folly of that.

---

39. 2 Stat. 132, 156 (1802).

Law professor Barry Friedman has stated that *Marbury* "is revered today both at home and abroad for establishing the Supreme Court's power of judicial review."[40] The Court's power of judicial review was established long before *Marbury,* however. Elements of Marshall's decision merit reverence, but which ones? That the Court is superior to the two elected branches? No. Some elements of the decision deserve praise, but not that one. There are many downsides to Marshall's action. Why did he even participate in the case? His previous position as Secretary of State and failure to deliver the commission to Marbury disqualified him. He should have recused himself. He could not possibly claim impartiality in handling the case. Writing in 2006, law professor Jeffrey Rosen noted: "By modern standards, he should never have agreed to hear the case in the first place."[41] One need not judge that question solely by contemporary legal principles. The standards in place in 1803 disqualified Marshall.

Marshall decided the Court lacked jurisdiction to hear the case. Marbury needed to begin in district court and take his case to the Supreme Court as part of its appellate jurisdiction. He had no grounds in Article III to bring the case under original jurisdiction. Having decided to dismiss the case on jurisdictional grounds, Marshall decided to use it to score some political points. He spent considerable time and space in lecturing Jefferson about improprieties: "To withhold his commission, therefore, is an act deemed by the

---

40. Barry Friedman, The Will of the People: How Public Opinion Has Influenced the Supreme Court and Shaped the Meaning of the Constitution 44 (2009).

41. Jeffrey Rosen, The Most Democratic Branch: How the Courts Serve America 22 (2006).

court not warranted by law, but violative of a vested legal right."[42] Barry Friedman remarked that this "gratuitous tongue-lashing of Jefferson and Madison for failing to deliver Marbury's commission was entirely unwarranted."[43] Political scientist Edward Corwin reached a similar judgment in 1914: "The Court was bent on reading the President a lecture on his legal and moral duty to recent Federalist appointees to judicial offices."[44] Many scholars interpreting this decision agree that everything Marshall said after deciding the Court lacked jurisdiction is "legally valueless."[45]

Why did Marshall speak disingenuously about Marbury's "right" to his job as justice of the peace in the District of Columbia? Marshall suggested that because Jefferson and Madison refused to deliver the commission to Marbury, he had a right to the job. Clearly that was false. On the basis on which Marshall decided the case, Marbury had no such right. Perhaps 90 percent of this decision is political, not legal. One of the illusions supporting judicial independence is the supposed separation between law and politics. Marshall's decision is largely political in its impulse and content.

If Marshall decided the Court lacked jurisdiction to hear and decide the case, why engage in such a lengthy opinion? One scholar observed: "The learned Justice really manufactured an opportunity to declare an act void."[46] Marshall spent

----

42. Marbury v. Madison, 5 U.S. (1 Cr.) 137, 162 (1803).

43. Friedman, The Will of the People, at 63.

44. Edward S. Corwin, "Marbury v. Madison and the Doctrine of Judicial Review," 12 Mich. L. Rev. 538, 543 (1914).

45. Andrew C. McLaughlin, "Marbury v. Madison Again," 14 Am. Bar Ass'n J. 155, 156 (1928).

46. Id. at 157.

time distinguishing between appellate and original jurisdiction, without much clarity of analysis. Certainly it can be argued that Congress may not reduce the Court's original jurisdiction. But why may it not add to it?[47] Another scholar concluded that Marshall's analysis of original and appellate jurisdiction amounted to "strained reading."[48]

Realizing that Madison and Jefferson would not carry out a Court order to deliver the commissions, Marshall decided to invalidate Section 13 of the Judiciary Act of 1789, which authorized the Court to issue writs of mandamus. He concluded that Section 13 expanded the Court's original jurisdiction and was thus invalid. His analysis of original and appellate jurisdiction is less than compelling, but it allowed him to avoid a confrontation with Jefferson that threatened to weaken the judiciary.

In subsequent years, Marshall regretted the way *Marbury* was being interpreted by lawyers. In *Cohens* v. *Virginia* (1821), he was troubled that his decision was being carelessly picked apart. He objected that litigants failed to separate the core of *Marbury* from its "*dicta.*"[49] To Marshall, the "single question" before the Court in 1803 was "whether the legislature could give this Court original jurisdiction in a case in which the constitution had clearly not given it."[50] That was the core holding. Everything else, including possible arguments for

---

47. Van Alstyne, "A Critical Guide to Marbury v. Madison," 1969 Duke L. J. at 15–16, 30–33.

48. Michael W. McConnell, "The Story of Marbury v. Madison," in Constitutional Law Stories 29 (Michael C. Dorf, ed., 2004).

49. Cohens v. Virginia, 19 U.S. (6 Wheat.) 264, 399 (1821) (emphasis in original).

50. Id. at 400.

judicial supremacy, amounts to dicta. He admitted that some of the language in *Marbury* was not only too broad "but in some instances contradictory to its principle."[51] Because Marshall disowned much of *Marbury,* it is impermissible to treat each sentence as constitutionally binding. One particular sentence deserves close scrutiny.

"Emphatically the Province"

Federal courts and scholars often cite the following sentence in *Marbury* to establish judicial supremacy: "It is emphatically the province and duty of the judicial department to say what the law is."[52] In 1958, the Supreme Court accepted a case involving Arkansas governor Orval Faubus's efforts to stop court-ordered integration of white and black schoolchildren. His action directly threatened the Court's desegregation ruling in *Brown* v. *Board of Education* (1954). Citing the "emphatically the province" sentence, the Court stated that *Marbury* "declared the basic principle that the federal judiciary is supreme in the exposition of the law of the Constitution, and that principle has ever since been respected by this Court and the Country as a permanent and indispensable feature of our constitutional system."[53]

How does that particular sentence in *Marbury* establish judicial supremacy? To clarify the sentence, it helps to remove some of the frills up front, producing a shortened version: "It is the duty of the judicial department to say what the law is."

---

51. Id. at 401.

52. Marbury v. Madison, 5 U.S. (1 Cr.) at 177.

53. Cooper v. Aaron, 358 U.S. 1, 18 (1958).

We might even use "courts" instead of "the judicial department," yielding: "It is the duty of courts to say what the law is." Even briefer: "Courts decide the law." The essence of the sentence is obvious, even trite. That is why courts are created. Nothing in the sentence says anything about judicial supremacy.

That conclusion is reinforced by rewriting the sentence in this manner: "It is emphatically the province and duty of Congress to say what the law is." No one would dispute the accuracy of that sentence, but it doesn't make Congress supreme either. Consider this rewrite: "It is emphatically the province and duty of the president to say what the law is." There is much truth in that sentence in terms of the president's power to exercise the veto and the duty of executive agencies to issue regulations to carry out statutory programs. Charles Hobson, a noted scholar on John Marshall, correctly states that the language "emphatically the province" does not imply "any claim to judicial supremacy in expounding the Constitution or to exclusive guardianship of the fundamental law."[54]

Further evidence that Marshall did not advocate judicial supremacy comes from a letter he sent to Justice Chase. *Marbury* was handed down on February 24, 1803. The House impeached Judge Pickering a week later, on March 2. The Senate convicted him on March 12, 1804. Congress then directed the impeachment machinery against Chase, making it clear that justices were proper targets. In a letter to Chase on January 23, 1805, Marshall made it quite clear that if members of Congress did not like a particular judicial opinion, it was not necessary to impeach a judge. Congress could simply pass a

---

54. Charles F. Hobson, The Great Chief Justice: John Marshall and the Rule of Law 67 (1996).

statute to override an objectionable decision. The letter begins by reviewing the doctrine of attaint and the related policy that a judge giving a legal opinion contrary to the position of the legislature is liable to impeachment. Marshall dated the letter January 23, 1804, but modern scholarship fixes the date a year later.[55] Like the rest of us, Marshall forgot to switch to the new year (see Box 1.3).

Marshall's letter scarcely carries the tone or substance of judicial supremacy. The words are not those of a headstrong justice determined to impose his will on elected officials. Instead, he recognizes the need and the propriety to share constitutional interpretation with Congress and the president. The judiciary is one of three coequal branches.

Two other issues in *Marbury* merit attention. Toward the end of his opinion, Marshall reminds the reader that he was required to strike down Section 13 because of his oath

---

Box 1.3

Marshall Writes to Chase

Jan. 23, 1805

My dear Sir ...

As, for convenience & humanity the old doctrine of attaint has yielded to the silent, moderate but not less operative influence of new trials, I think the modern doctrine of impeachment shoud [sic] yield to an appellate jurisdiction in the legislature. A reversal of those legal opinions deemd [sic] unsound by the legislature would certainly better comport with the mildness of our character than [would] a removal of the Judge who has rendered them unknowing of his fault.

J. Marshall

Source: 3 Albert J. Beveridge, The Life of John Marshall 177 (1919).

---

55. 6 The Papers of John Marshall 348 n.1 (Hobson, ed., 1990).

of office: "Why otherwise does [the Constitution] direct the judges to take an oath to support it? This oath certainly applies in an especial manner, to their conduct in their official character." He said it would be "immoral" to impose the oath on judges "if they were to be used as the instruments, and the knowing instruments, for violating what they swear to support!"[56] Marshall went far afield with his rhetoric. Members of Congress, the president, state judges, and other public officials take an oath to defend the Constitution. The ceremony of oath-taking does not give the Court the final word.

Marshall had a capacity to present a conclusion as though no other alternative could possibly exist. In *Marbury* he wrote: "It is a proposition too plain to be contested, that the constitution controls any legislative act repugnant to it; or, that the legislature may alter the constitution by an ordinary act.... The constitution is either a superior paramount law, unchangeable by ordinary means, or it is on a level with ordinary legislative acts, and, like other acts, is alterable when the legislature shall please to alter it."[57] That may sound plausible, even indisputable, but if a statute contrary to the Constitution may not stand, why tolerate a Supreme Court decision that is contrary to the Constitution? Legal scholar Nelson Lund asked: "[I]f statutes enacted by the people's representatives are always trumped by the Constitution, it would seem to follow by inexorable logic that mere judicial opinions must also be trumped by the Constitution."[58]

---

56. Marbury v. Madison, 5 U.S. (1 Cr.) at 180.

57. Id. at 177.

58. Nelson Lund, "Resolved, Presidential Signing Statements Threaten to Undermine the Rule of Law and the Separation of Power" (con), in Richard J. Ellis & Michael Nelson, eds., Debating the Presidency: Conflicting Perspectives on the American Executive 150 (2010).

Another Possible Collision

Marbury concerned the statute passed by the Federalists creating new justices of the peace. A second lawsuit involved the Circuit Court Act passed to form sixteen new lifetime judgeships. After taking power, the Jeffersonians repealed that statute. Did Congress possess authority to do that? Many Federalists found it constitutionally repugnant for Congress to not only take a judge out of office (except by impeachment) but to take the office out of the judge. This second lawsuit provides important insights into Marshall's attitude about judicial supremacy. Regrettably, courts and scholars place great emphasis on *Marbury* but give little attention to this second case.

The constitutionality of the repeal statute reached the Court in *Stuart* v. *Laird*. Opponents of the repeal argued in favor of judicial independence: "The words *during good behavior* can not mean *during the will of Congress*. The people have a right to the services of those judges who have been constitutionally appointed; and who have been unconstitutionally removed from office."[59] At issue for the Court, however, was not a mere matter of law. If the justices exercised judicial review by striking down the repeal statute, they knew it would greatly intensify congressional efforts to impeach and remove Federalist judges. Marshall was not directly involved. He had tried *Stuart* in the court below and disqualified himself when the Supreme Court acted.[60] Still, he had a responsibility to protect not only the Court, but the entire federal judiciary.

---

59. Stuart v. Laird, 5 U.S. (1 Cr.) 299, 304 (1803) (emphasis in original).

60. Id. at 308.

Stuart was decided on March 2, 1803—a week after *Marbury*. No doubt many of the justices were offended by having the new circuit courts eliminated, forcing them to ride circuit once again. Would they invoke the supposed new power of *Marbury* to strike down the repeal statute? That thought must have been tempting. However, beyond the likely congressional counterattack if the Court found the repeal unconstitutional was the Court's credibility. In 1789, Congress created circuit courts that were a mix of district judges and Supreme Court justices. Justices had ridden circuit from 1789 to 1803 and no one had raised a constitutional objection. Both law and prudence required the Court to defer to the legislative judgment. Said the Court in *Stuart*: "It is sufficient to observe, that practice and acquiescence under it for a period of several years, commencing with the organization of the judicial system, affords an irresistable [sic] answer, and has indeed fixed the construction." The congressional judgment represented "a contemporary interpretation of the most forcible nature. This practical exposition is too strong and obstinate to be shaken or controlled."[61] Who fixed the construction? Congress. Whose constitutional interpretation prevailed? Congress's. The final voice on this constitutional issue went to the elected branches.

After *Marbury* was decided, Jefferson wrote to Mrs. John Adams in 1804: "You seem to think it devolved on the judges to decide on the validity of the sedition law [of 1798]. But nothing in the Constitution has given them a right to decide for the Executive, more than to the Executive to decide for them." In articulating this doctrine of coordinate construction, Jefferson concluded that each branch was "independent in the sphere of action assigned to them." Judges could fine

61. Id. at 309.

and imprison someone, but the president possessed an independent power to pardon the individual. Giving judges the exclusive power to decide questions of constitutionality, he said, "would make the judiciary a despotic branch."[62]

The manner in which the Court decided *Stuart*—deferring to congressional judgment—would be repeated many times. Under British common law, individuals could be punished under the doctrine of "seditious libel" even when no statute existed. Would that legal precedent be applied in the United States? A case that reached the Supreme Court in 1812 involved editors of a Federalist newspaper in Connecticut. The Jefferson administration prosecuted them under the doctrine of seditious libel. The Court noted that this was the first time it faced the issue of whether federal courts had jurisdiction over seditious libel. Would it settle the question unilaterally under the theory that it held some kind of exclusive authority over legal and constitutional questions? No. It announced that the issue had "been long since settled in public opinion," by which it meant that Congress, following the expiration of the Sedition Act in 1801, had yet to establish by statute a successor. Congress refused to pass legislation making it a criminal act to criticize the national government. In other words, constitutional law was decided by the people working through their elected representatives. Whatever precedents existed in England, the exercise of criminal jurisdiction in common law cases was a matter for Congress to decide. It was not within the implied power of federal courts.[63]

---

62. 11 The Writings of Thomas Jefferson 51 (Bergh, ed., 1904).

63. United States v. Hudson and Goodwin, 11 U.S. (7 Cr.) 32 (1812). See also United States v. Coolidge, 14 U.S. (1 Wheat.) 415 (1816) and Leonard W. Levy, Jefferson and Civil Liberties: The Darker Side 42–69 (1963).

Marshall's Contribution

Chief Justice Marshall's decision in *Marbury* has been described "as a masterful closely-reasoned document."[64] It can scarcely be called that, but it does merit praise because Marshall protected the independence and continued health of the judiciary. In 1803, the national judiciary was very much an endangered branch. The Federalist Party had been severely weakened by the John Adams administration and the Alien and Sedition Acts. The party continued to lose power until it passed out of existence. Constitutional scholar Michael McConnell expressed it well: "*Marbury* was brilliant, then, not for its effective assertion of judicial power, but for its effective avoidance of judicial humiliation."[65]

Although *Marbury* is correctly remembered as the first time the Court struck down a congressional statute, we need to remember that Marshall never again invalidated legislation by Congress. Quite the contrary. He did not try to elevate the judiciary over the elected branches. That would have been unsuccessful and damaging to the courts. Instead, judicial review became a means of affirming—not invalidating—congressional judgments on constitutional matters. As noted by Jean Edward Smith in his biographical study, Marshall in *Marbury* "was neither embarking on a crusade for judicial supremacy, nor was he charting new territory.... Read in its entirety, *Marbury* v. *Madison* is an essay on the necessity for moderation."[66]

---

64. Irwin S. Rhodes, "Marbury Versus Madison Revisited," 33 U. Cinc. L. Rev. 23, 225 (1964).

65. McConnell, *supra* note 48, at 31.

66. Jean Edward Smith, John Marshall: Definer of a Nation 326 (1998).

The active forces in developing new constitutional doctrines during his years on the Court were Congress and the
president, not the judiciary. Lawmakers decided to create the
First Bank of the United States (aka U.S. Bank) and exercise
their commerce power. On each occasion Marshall was there
to bestow a judicial blessing and lend legitimacy to statutory
policy. In a series of rulings, he fortified national power over
the states. Writing in 1911, Louis Boudin concluded that
Marshall's "great place in the history of our country" results
not from *Marbury,* which over the years produced many claims
of "doubtful warrant," but from "the liberal spirit in which
he interpreted, and thus helped to develop, the legislative
powers of Congress."[67]

The most outlandish and erroneous praise for *Marbury*
came from the Supreme Court in 1958 when it ruled against
the efforts of Governor Faubus to block the integration of
public schools in Little Rock, Arkansas. The Court claimed
that the decision in 1803 "declared the basic principle that
the federal judiciary is supreme in the exposition of the law
of the Constitution, and that principle has ever since been
respected by this Court and the Country as the permanent and
indispensable feature of our constitutional system."[68] Nothing in that sentence is true. The Court has not respected that
principle, nor have the elected branches or the public. If that
principle had any substance the nation would have accepted
such Court rulings as *Dred Scott* in 1857, the Court's "separate
but equal" doctrine of 1896, the child-labor cases of 1918 and
1922, the first flag-salute case of 1940, the Japanese American

---

67. L. B. Boudin, "Government by Judiciary," 26 Pol. Sci. Q. 238,
256 (1911).

68. Cooper v. Aaron, 358 U.S. 1, 18 (1958).

these were accepted until modifying legislation approved by the Court

cases of 1943 and 1944, the trimester framework of *Roe* v. *Wade,* the yarmulke case of 1986, and many other Court rulings that were repudiated by Congress and the public. All of those examples are discussed in detail in subsequent chapters.

Statutory Limits on Judicial Review

By adopting specific language in statutes, Congress can prohibit judicial review for certain types of cases. For example, legislation in 1885 stated that decisions by accounting officers in the Treasury Department regarding claims for property were to be treated as final determinations "and shall never thereafter be reopened or reconsidered." A unanimous Court held that the statute conferred exclusive and final jurisdiction on the Treasury Department and that federal courts had no authority to exercise judicial review over the agency's judgment.[69] Most decisions by the Secretary of Veterans Affairs on "questions of law and fact" affecting veterans' benefits "shall be final and conclusive and may not be reviewed by any other official or by any court."[70] The Supreme Court accepts the prohibition on judicial review on these questions of benefits and claims, providing there is no constitutional issue.[71] Legislation in 1988 subjected certain actions by the Department of Veterans Affairs to judicial review. Under that authority, the Court decided a veterans' case in 1994.[72]

69. United States v. Babcock, 250 U.S. 328 (1919).
70. 38 U.S.C. § 511.
71. Johnson v. Robison, 415 U.S. 361, 366–67 (1974).
72. 102 Stat. 4105 (1988); Brown v. Gardner, 513 U.S. 115 (1994).

The Administrative Procedure Act (APA) prohibits judicial review over actions "committed to agency discretion by law."[73] When the Supreme Court determines that an agency action falls within that scope, it acknowledges that judicial review does not apply.[74] Congress may authorize the Attorney General to make temporary orders that are not subject to judicial review.[75] The Defense Base Closure and Realignment Act of 1990 established a commission to recommend the closing of unnecessary military bases. A unanimous Court in 1994 ruled that the commission recommendations were not a "final agency action" under the APA because the ultimate decision on closure rests with the president. Therefore the recommendations are not reviewable by the courts. The Court noted: "Where a statute, such as the 1990 Act, commits decision-making to the discretion of the President, judicial review of the President's action is not available."[76] Two years earlier, the Court held that certain presidential actions are not reviewable under the APA because the president is not an "agency."[77]

A Public Conversation on Constitutional Law

The framers never intended to vest in the Court final and exclusive authority over the meaning of the Constitution. The Court has never exercised such unchecked power. Edward Corwin wrote in 1938: "The juristic conception of judicial

---

73. 5 U.S.C. § 701(a)(2).

74. Lincoln v. Vigil, 508 U.S. 182 (1993).

75. Touby v. United States, 500 U.S. 160 (1991).

76. Dalton v. Specter, 511 U.S. 462, 477 (1994).

77. Franklin v. Massachusetts, 505 U.S. 788 (1992).

review invokes a miracle. It supposes a kind of transubstantiation whereby the Court's opinion of the Constitution, if pertinent to the decision of the case properly before the Court, becomes the very blood and body of the Constitution."[78] Before joining the Court, Felix Frankfurter advised President Franklin D. Roosevelt: "People have been taught to believe that when the Supreme Court speaks it is not they who speak but the Constitution, whereas, of course, in so many vital cases, it is *they* who speak and not the Constitution."[79] Justice Byron White remarked in a dissenting opinion in 1970: "This Court is not alone in being obliged to construe the Constitution in the course of its work; nor does it even approach having a monopoly on the wisdom and insight appropriate to the task."[80]

Writing in 1962, Yale law professor Alexander Bickel emphasized that courts find themselves engaged in a "continuing dialogue" with political institutions and society at large, a process in which constitutional principle is "evolved conversationally not perfected unilaterally."[81] A purely technical analysis of court rulings misses the constant, creative, and constructive interplay between the judiciary and the political system. The Supreme Court is not the sole or even the dominant agency in resolving constitutional questions.

---

78. Edward S. Corwin, "What Kind of Judicial Review Did the Framers Have in Mind?," 86 Pittsburgh L. J. 4, 15 (1938). The published version incorrectly used the first name "Edwin."

79. Max Freedman, anno., Roosevelt and Frankfurter: Their Correspondence 383 (1967) (emphasis in original).

80. Welsh v. United States, 398 U.S. 333, 370 (1970) (White, J., dissenting).

81. Alexander M. Bickel, The Least Dangerous Branch: The Supreme Court at the Bar of Politics 240, 244 (1962).

CHAPTER TWO
HOW THE COURT DECIDES

Questions of judicial organization ultimately present questions of power. Congress has the power to create and monitor the federal court system. The president has the power to nominate judges and the Senate has the power to confirm them. Nomination and confirmation bring many individuals and interest groups into the process. In a formal sense, the president nominates judges. In practice, he shares that task with many other individuals, particularly U.S. senators. Other issues of judicial tenure, removal, and compensation add to political conflicts.

Creating Federal Courts

The framers understood how the concept of judicial independence developed in England. The Act of Settlement, passed by England in 1701, guaranteed tenure for judges during good behavior. Still, kings and queens had substantial authority over the British courts. In the American colonies, the power to constitute courts was vested in the governor and council (creatures of the king). The legislative assemblies were permitted to create courts for small causes, subject always to the king's veto.[1]

The importance of judicial independence occupies several sections of the Declaration of Independence. The American framers accused the king of "obstruct[ing] the Administration of Justice, by refusing his Assent to Laws for establishing Judiciary Powers." Because of disputes between the British Crown and the American colonies, laws establishing courts of justices were repeatedly struck down, often eliminating courts for long stretches of time.[2] The Declaration rebuked the king for making judges "dependent on his Will alone, for the Tenure of their Offices, and the Amount and Payment of Their Salaries." The policy of having colonial judges serve at the king's pleasure provoked bitter objections in New York, New Jersey, Pennsylvania, North Carolina, South Carolina, and Massachusetts, where colonial legislatures wanted judges to have tenure during good behavior.[3] Following the break with England, several American colonies included tenure and salary provisions in their constitutions to secure judicial independence.

After the colonies separated from England, state governments authorized vessels to prey on British shipping. A judicial system was needed to adjudicate "prizes" (property captured at sea). State admiralty courts made the initial judgment, but appeals beyond that level required action by the Continental Congress. From 1776 to 1780, appeals were handled first by temporary legislative committees and then by a standing

---

1. 1 Julius Goebel, Jr., History of the Supreme Court of the United States: Antecedents and Beginnings 12–13 (1971).

2. Edmund Dumbauld, The Declaration of Independence and What It Means Today 108–12 (1950).

3. Id. at 112–15.

committee, until Congress, in May 1780, created a Court of Appeals in Cases of Capture. This tribunal, the first national judiciary, took direction from the Continental Congress and even from the Secretary for Foreign Affairs.[4] During that period, the Court of Appeals and executive officers served as agents of Congress. Separate judicial and executive branches did not exist. The Court of Appeals continued to function when delegates arrived in Philadelphia in May 1787 to draft a new constitution.

As explained in Chapter One, the delegates explored the possibility of a Council of Revision but eventually eliminated it. Article III of the Constitution created a separate judicial branch, with federal judges holding their office "during good Behaviour," with salaries that could not be diminished. Article III expressly recognizes the Supreme Court, but the number and types of inferior courts were left to Congress, with authority to establish them "from time to time." The legislative creation of lower courts was purely discretionary. Some members of the First United States Congress considered doing only the minimum: staff and fund the Supreme Court but rely on the states for trial courts. Madison warned that courts in many states "cannot be trusted with the execution of Federal laws." Because of limited tenure and possible salary reductions, some state courts were too dependent on their legislatures. Making federal laws depend on state courts, he said, "would throw us back into all the embarrassments which characterized our former situation."[5] Congress decided to create federal district courts.

---

4. Id. at 178–79; see Henry J. Bourguignon, The First Federal Court: The Federal Appellate Prize Court of the American Revolution (1977).

5. 1 Annals of Cong. 812–13 (1789).

The Judiciary Act of 1789 provided for a chief justice and five associate justices for the Supreme Court. It divided the United States into thirteen districts, with a federal judge for each district. It created three circuits to handle appellate cases: the eastern, middle, and southern circuits. Circuit courts, meeting twice a year in each district, consisted of any two justices of the Supreme Court and one district judge from that circuit. District judges could not vote in any case of appeal from their own decision. Section 25 of the Judiciary Act solidified federal control over the states by giving the Supreme Court a supervisory role over state courts.

Supreme Court justices complained bitterly about their circuit-court duties. Forced to "ride circuit" around the country to hear appellate cases exposed the justices to arduous and hazardous travel. Moreover, a justice might have to review his own decision if the case reached the Supreme Court. The option at that point would be recusal, reducing the Court by one justice on those cases. All six justices appealed to President George Washington and Congress to reduce their labors. Legislation in 1793 changed the mix for the circuit courts to consist of one justice and two district judges.

The next step was the controversial circuit court Judiciary Act of 1801, passed in the remaining days of the Adams administration. It promised to terminate circuit-riding by establishing sixteen circuit judges for six circuits. As detailed in Chapter One, the Jeffersonians repealed that statute, an action upheld by the Supreme Court in *Stuart* v. *Laird* (1803). The Judiciary Act of 1801 also reduced the number of justices from six to five, effective with the next vacancy. The reduction might have been justified because the work of the Court had been reduced by eliminating circuit duties. Also, having five justices avoided the possibility of tie votes. Jeffersonians interpreted the statute less charitably. It decreased Jefferson's opportunity to appoint his own candidate to the High Court.

A major step in judicial reorganization occurred in 1891 when Congress created a separate system of appellate courts, producing three tiers: district (trial) courts, circuit (appellate) courts, and the Supreme Court. A comprehensive "Judges Bill" in 1925 gave the Supreme Court greater discretion to grant or deny petitions of appeals from lower courts. Currently, the Court receives about 8,000 petitions for review each year. Out of that volume, the Court issues fewer than eighty decisions a year, half of what it did in the 1980s.[6] A few cases concern original jurisdiction and are placed on the "original docket." Original jurisdiction is used sparingly to protect the Court's principal work with its appellate docket. To assist in the handling of its original jurisdiction, the Court typically appoints special masters to study an issue and present recommendations. Congress passed legislation in 1988 to substantially reduce the Court's mandatory or obligatory jurisdiction.[7]

Thresholds for Judicial Action

The scope of judicial review is circumscribed by rules of self-restraint fashioned by judges. Certain thresholds (also called gatekeeping rules) shield judges from cases they do not want to hear, at times to ration scarce judicial resources and avoid politically sensitive questions. When federal courts decline to

---

6. Louis Fisher & Katy J. Harriger, American Constitutional Law 162 (10th ed., 2013).

7. 102 Stat. 662 (1988).

take a case, the resolution of constitutional issues falls to the elected branches and the states. In 1821, Chief Justice John Marshall suggested fixed boundaries for judicial action: "It is most true that this Court will not take jurisdiction if it should not: but it is equally true, that it must take jurisdiction if it should."[8] In fact, what the Court should or should not accept is largely a matter of judicial discretion. Reflecting on his work at the Supreme Court, Justice Louis Brandeis noted, "The most important thing we do is not doing."[9]

In a concurrence in a 1936 decision, Brandeis summarized the rules used by the Supreme Court to limit its exercise of judicial review. Known as the Ashwander Rules, they stated that the Court should not anticipate a question of constitutional law in advance of the necessity of deciding it and should not formulate a rule of constitutional law broader than what is required by the particular case.[10] Those are sound principles, but not always followed. Another rule: "The Court will not pass upon the validity of a statute upon complaint of one who fails to show that he is injured by its operation." The Court also insists that the dispute be real and not contrived, with parties on each side ready to inform the Court through the adversary process. Occasionally the Court fails to follow that rule.[11] An example is the mandatory-sterilization case *Buck v. Bell* (1927), covered in Chapter Three.

---

8. Cohens v. Virginia, 6 Wheat. 264, 404 (1821).

9. Alexander M. Bickel, The Unpublished Opinions of Mr. Justice Brandeis 17 (1957).

10. Ashwander v. TVA, 297 U.S. 288 (1936).

11. Buck v. Bell, 274 U.S. 200 (1927). Explaining why this case was a "friendly suit": Paul A. Lombardo, "Three Generations, No Imbeciles: New Light on Buck v. Bell," 60 N.Y.U. L. Rev. 30 (1985).

To resolve a legal claim, courts need to know that parties have been adversely affected. Abstract or hypothetical questions, removed from a concrete factual setting, prevent courts from reaching an informed judgment. Legal questions need to be addressed "in an adversary context and in a form historically viewed as capable of resolution through the judicial process."[12] By acting through the adversary process, judges and juries can seek truth by hearing two sets of advocates present their case. This procedure assumes that two antagonistic parties, each with a sufficient stake in the outcome, will marshal the best arguments to defend their interests.

Courts occasionally consider a case even when both parties take the same position on the legal issue. In the 1940s, three federal employees went to court to challenge a provision in an appropriations bill they regarded as a forbidden bill of attainder. The Justice Department agreed with their judgment. For the Court to insist on two rival parties would have left the employees without a legal remedy. To protect its interests in the suit, Congress passed legislation to create a special counsel, who functioned officially as *amicus curiae* but provided sufficient adverseness to allow the case to proceed. The Supreme Court held in favor of the three employees.[13]

To satisfy the requirements of a case capable of being decided by federal courts, parties bringing an action must have standing to sue. "Generalizations about standing to sue," Justice William Douglas once said with customary bluntness, "are largely worthless as such."[14] Some generalizations, however, are helpful. To demonstrate standing, parties must

---

12. Flast v. Cohen, 392 U.S. 83, 95 (1968).
13. United States v. Lovett, 328 U.S. 303 (1946).
14. Data Processing Service v. Camp, 397 U.S. 150, 151 (1970).

show injury to a legally protected interest, an injury that is real rather than abstract or hypothetical. Injuries may be economic and noneconomic. They may be actual or threatened. Injuries may affect either organizations or persons. In 1992, the Supreme Court identified three main elements of standing (see Box 2.1).

Litigants able to establish standing at the outset of a case may find their personal stake diluted or eliminated by subsequent events. Because of a change in law or facts, there may be insufficient adverseness to guide the court. If the initial action that triggered the complaint ceases, a court may have no means of granting relief. At that point the case becomes moot and is dismissed. Just as a case brought too late can be moot, a case brought too early may not yet be "ripe." Many cases raising constitutional issues are avoided by courts on grounds of mootness and lack of ripeness.

Box 2.1

Elements of Standing

Over the years, our cases have established that the irreducible constitutional minimum of standing contains three elements. First, the plaintiff must have suffered an "injury in fact"—an invasion of a legally protected interest which is (a) concrete and particularized . . . and (b) "actual or imminent, not 'conjectural' or 'hypothetical.'" . . . Second, there must be a causal connection between the injury and the conduct complained of—the injury has to be "fairly trace[able] to the challenged action of the defendant, and not . . . th[e] result [of] the independent action of some third party not before the court." . . . Third, it must be "likely," as opposed to merely "speculative," that the injury will be "redressed by a favorable decision."

Source: Lujan v. Defenders of Wildlife, 504 U.S. 555, 560–6 (1992).

Political Questions

Another method for courts to sidestep a legal and constitutional dispute is to call it a "political question." This doctrine
depends in part on circular reasoning. Chief Justice Marshall
insisted in *Marbury* v. *Madison* that "questions in their nature
political ... can never be made in this court."[15] Yet every
question that reaches a court is, by its very nature, political.
Justice Oliver Wendell Holmes, Jr., hearing a litigant claim
that a question concerning a party primary could not be
addressed in court because of its political character, rejected
the objection as "little more than a play upon words."[16] In
1962, the Supreme Court identified six areas that are generally classified as political questions.[17] The categories are very
broad and provide only rough guidance for the courts.[18]

There are many examples of courts avoiding constitutional issues that are resolved by the elected branches.[19] Here
is a contemporary example. After the Supreme Court dismissed a constitutional dispute under the standing doctrine,
it was confronted and settled years later by lawmakers and the
president. In 1974, the Court denied standing to a taxpayer
who challenged the constitutionality of covert spending by
the Central Intelligence Agency. Congress did not provide
funds directly to the agency. Funds were hidden in appropriations accounts. Upon enactment, the appropriations were
allocated to the CIA, which made no public statement of its

---

15. 5 U.S. (1 Cr.) 137, 170 (1803).

16. Nixon v. Herndon, 273 U.S. 536, 540 (1927).

17. Baker v. Carr, 369 U.S. 186 (1962).

18. Fisher & Harriger, *supra* note 6, at 101–11.

19. E.g., Louis Fisher, "Separation of Powers: Interpretation Outside
the Courts," 18 Pepperdine L. Rev. 57 (1990).

expenditures. This budgetary procedure violated a provision in Article I, Section 9: "A regular Statement and Account of the Receipts and Expenditures of all public Money shall be published from time to time."

In 1997, under pressure of a lawsuit by a private citizen, the CIA released a figure of $26.6 billion for the entire intelligence community, which consists of the CIA, the National Security Agency, and many other agencies. Of that amount, the CIA portion was about $3 billion. The next year, the CIA released a figure of $26.7 billion for the intelligence community but thereafter refused to disclose any budgetary figures. In 2007, Congress passed legislation requiring the administration to disclose the aggregate budget of the intelligence community.[20] Each year the aggregate amount is publicly disclosed. The current total is approximately $80 billion.

Appointing Judges

The delegates at the Philadelphia Convention rejected the British system of an exclusive executive power to appoint, associating it with official corruption and debasement of the judiciary. At first they placed the power to select judges solely with Congress. Next they considered vesting that responsibility solely with the Senate. Only late in the convention did they settle on joint action by the president and the Senate.[21] Under Article II, Section 2, of the Constitution, the president "shall nominate, and by and with the Advice and

---

20. 121 Stat. 35 (2007).
21. 1 Farrand 21, 63, 119–28, 232–33; 2 Farrand 41–44, 80–83, 121.

Consent of the Senate, shall appoint . . . Judges of the supreme Court." The Constitution also authorizes Congress to vest the appointment of "inferior Officers" in the president alone, in the courts, or in the heads of the executive departments. In addition, there is the possibility of the president making unilateral recess appointments, discussed later in this chapter.

At face value, the Constitution appears to give the president the exclusive power to nominate ("he shall nominate"). Technically, nominations come only from the president. However, many public officials and private citizens participate actively and influentially in the pre-nomination process.[22] From the beginning, senators wield nearly exclusive power in choosing nominees for district courts and at times for circuit courts. Typically they submit two or three names for a judgeship, allowing the president some choice. When Senator John Warner sent three names to President George H. W. Bush for a vacant federal judgeship in Virginia's Western District and two names for a vacancy in the Eastern District, a headline in a newspaper read, "Warner Nominates 5 for Judgeships."[23] On occasion, senators have had a dominant influence in the selection of a justice. Members of the Supreme Court, such as Chief Justice William Howard Taft, exercised a prominent role. The American Bar Association has played an important function in evaluating potential judicial nominees. Presidents established nominating panels to recommend five candidates for each judicial vacancy, allowing the president to make the final choice. Senators wield a number of potent tools in

---

22. Mitchel A. Sollenberger, The President Shall Nominate: How Congress Trumps Executive Power (2008).

23. "Warner Nominates 5 for Judgeships," Washington Post, March 12, 1989, at B3.

controlling judicial appointments, ranging from filibusters to Senate "holds" and the use of "blue slips" to effectively block committee action on a judicial nominee.[24]

The Senate has refused to confirm almost one-fifth of presidential nominations to the Supreme Court. Twenty-five nominees have been rejected, had their names submitted without Senate action, or been forced to withdraw. Most of those actions (eighteen) occurred before 1900. John Parker, nominated to the Supreme Court in 1930, was defeated in a Senate vote. In recent times, the Senate in 1968 refused to advance Associate Justice Abe Fortas to the position of chief justice. Fortas, subjected to embarrassing questions about his acceptance of fees from private parties, eventually asked President Lyndon Johnson to withdraw his nomination. There was widespread criticism of his close friendship with Johnson and frequent meetings with him, which created an aura of cronyism. A year later, with impeachment proceedings gearing up against him, Fortas resigned from the Court. Other recent nominees who failed to be confirmed include Clement Haynsworth (rejected by the Senate in 1969), G. Harrold Carswell (rejected in 1970), and Robert Bork (rejected in 1987). Nominations not acted upon by the Senate include Douglas Ginsburg in 1988 and Harriet Miers in 2005.

Bork's rejection has received much commentary. As former Solicitor General and judge on the D.C. Circuit, he appeared to be eminently qualified for the position of associate justice. Why did his nomination fail? In part it was Bork's penchant for talking at great length, despite the constant advice from the White House to keep his answers

---

24. Mitchel A. Sollenberger, *Judicial Appointments and Democratic Controls* (2011).

short. Joe Biden, chairman of the Senate Judiciary Committee, would frequently remark: "I'm sorry, Judge Bork, did I interrupt you? Did you have something else you wanted to say?" And off Bork would go, opening up other problems for himself. He seemed intent on demonstrating that he was much smarter than the senators on the committee—perhaps an understandable desire, but one that did not improve his chances of being confirmed.

Bork's greatest error was to ridicule privacy as a constitutional right. That, too, was understandable, because Bork often enjoyed making fun of the Supreme Court's decision in *Griswold* v. *Connecticut* (1965), which struck down a state law banning contraceptives. Several passages in *Griswold* are easy to deride, such as Justice Douglas saying that the specific guarantees in the Bill of Rights "have penumbras, formed by emanations from those guarantees that help give them life and substance."[25] But the constitutional right to privacy was not a laughing matter. Although the word *privacy* does not appear in the U.S. Constitution, it does appear in a number of state constitutions and it is implied in the U.S. Constitution. There must be a point where government power stops and individual liberty is preserved.

As the hearing progressed and after Bork's prospects had dimmed, he testified that the Constitution "protects privacy in a variety of ways" (see Box 2.2).

Bork's admission came too late. Fifty-eight senators voted against his confirmation. No other nominee to the Supreme Court chose to repeat Bork's error. During Anthony Kennedy's associate justice confirmation hearing on December 14, 1987, the Senate Judiciary Committee asked whether certain

---

25. 381 U.S. 479, 484 (1965).

> ## Box 2.2
>
> ### Bork Acknowledges the Right of Privacy
>
> No civilized person wants to live in a society without a lot of privacy in it. And the framers, in fact, of the Constitution protected privacy in a variety of ways.
>
> The first amendment protects free exercise of religion. The free speech provision of the first amendment has been held to protect the privacy of membership lists and a person's associations in order to make the free speech right effective. The fourth amendment protects the individual's home and office from unreasonable searches and seizures, and usually requires a warrant. The fifth amendment has a right against self-incrimination.
>
> *Source:* "Nomination of Robert H. Bork to Be Associate Justice of the Supreme Court of the United States," hearings before the Senate Committee on the Judiciary, 100th Cong., 1st Sess. 241 (1987).

unenumerated rights, including the right to privacy, have a constitutional basis in the word "liberty" that appears in the Fifth and Fourteenth Amendments. Kennedy agreed: "There is a zone of liberty, a zone of protection, a line that is drawn where the individual can tell the Government: Beyond this line you may not go."[26] Kennedy was asked if the existence of unenumerated rights includes the right to privacy. He replied: "It seems to me that most Americans, most lawyers, most judges, believe that liberty includes protection of a value we call privacy."[27]

Another guideline for nominating justices comes from presidents who say they will select only individuals dedicated

---

26. "Nomination of Anthony M. Kennedy to Be Associate Justice of the Supreme Court of the United States," hearings before the Senate Committee on the Judiciary, 100th Cong., 1st Sess. 86 (1987).

27. Id. at 88.

to "strict constructionism," a standard that lacks any concrete meaning. Apparently these announcements are intended to convince the public and the Senate that the nominee will follow a constrained path once on the Court, but judges have widely different views on how to construe the Constitution and laws.[28]

Public Hearings

Confirmation hearings for Supreme Court justices offer an excellent opportunity to educate the American public. The discussion between nominees and senators should deepen our understanding of the Constitution and how it is interpreted. The hearings seldom deliver on that promise, however. Nominees, perhaps recalling Bork's rejection, are excessively cautious and prefer to deliver bland generalities. That is not necessary.

At his confirmation hearing in 1987, Anthony Kennedy willingly engaged in thoughtful dialogues with senators. The previous year, Senator Arlen Specter asked William Rehnquist, nominee for chief justice, whether he believed the Court was "the final arbiter, the final decisionmaker of what the Constitution means." Rehnquist, well aware that the question merited a thoughtful reply, decided to give a one-word answer: "Unquestionably."[29] He may have decided

---

28. For an excellent analysis of these theories, including the Living Constitution, Moral Reading, Textualism, Originalism, Political Process, Cost-Benefit Pragmatism, and Minimalism, see J. Harvie Wilkinson III, Cosmic Constitutional Theory: Why Americans Are Losing Their Inalienable Right to Self-Governance (2012).

29. "Nomination of Justice William Hubbs Rehnquist," hearings before the Senate Committee on the Judiciary, 99th Cong., 2d Sess. 187 (1986).

a more thorough and truthful answer might create problems for his confirmation.[30] Kennedy refused to duck the question with a single word. He explained that in such areas as separation of powers, changes in the growth in the office of the presidency, and in "the shape of federalism," Congress was far more powerful and authoritative than the Court.[31] He added, "I am somewhat reluctant to say that in all circumstances each legislator is immediately bound by the full consequences of a Supreme Court decree."[32]

Pressed on how he could make such a statement, Kennedy provided instructive details. He offered a hypothetical example. Suppose the Supreme Court were to overrule its decision in *New York Times Co.* v. *Sullivan,* removing from newspapers the immunity they had enjoyed from libel lawsuits. To Kennedy, lawmakers could say the new ruling was "constitutionally wrong" and decide to pass legislation to restore immunity and protect the freedom of the press. He advised: "I think you could stand up on the floor of the U.S. Senate and say I am introducing this legislation because in my view the Supreme Court of the United States is 180 degrees wrong under the Constitution. And I think you would be fulfilling your duty if you said that."[33] It seemed to him that "in some instances Congress is better off standing on its own feet and making its position known, and then its strength in the federal system will be greater than if it had relied on the

---

30. Rehnquist's capacity to think carefully about the forces that shape constitutional doctrine is reflected in his writings, such as "Constitutional Law and Public Opinion," 20 Suffolk U. L. Rev. 751 (1986).

31. *Supra* note 26, at 221.

32. Id. at 222.

33. Id. at 222–23; New York Times Co. v. Sullivan, 376 U.S. 254 (1964).

assistance of the courts."[34] Through these remarks he point-edly rejected judicial supremacy and displayed an understand-ing and respect for a rich constitutional dialogue among all three branches, or what is called coordinate construction.

In 2005, after being nominated as chief justice, John Roberts presented a short prepared statement at his confirma-tion hearing. He said that judges are "like umpires. Umpires don't make the rules; they apply them." His job was "to call balls and strikes."[35] Several senators remarked on his baseball analogy,[36] but without exploring it in any depth. In baseball, the strike zone is defined by the width of the home plate and the batter's height from the shoulders down to the knees. The U.S. Constitution has some clear strike zones, including a two-thirds majority for veto overrides, the age of at least thirty-five to be president, a six-year term for senators, and the requirement of two witnesses to prove treason. What is the strike zone for the equal protection of the laws, freedom of speech, free exercise of religion, due process of law, "unrea-sonable" searches and seizures, "cruel and unusual" punish-ments, and other constitutional issues that come regularly to the Supreme Court? There is none.

On June 30, 2010, at her confirmation hearing to be associate justice, Elena Kagan was asked about the baseball

---

34. Id. at 225.

35. His prepared statement can be watched at www.c-spanvideo.org /program/188437-1, beginning at 3:29:32. Accessed March 12, 2013.

36. "Confirmation Hearing on the Nomination of John G. Roberts, Jr. to Be Chief Justice of the United States," hearing before the Senate Committee on the Judiciary, 109th Cong., 1st Sess. 46, 184–86, 256–57, 279 (2005). Roberts's remarks about judges being like umpires, calling balls and strikes, appears at 55–56.

analogy. Regarding it as correct in some respects, she cautioned that "like all metaphors, it does have its limits." She expressed concern that it "might suggest to some people that law is a kind of robotic enterprise, that there is a kind of automatic quality to it, that it's easy, that we just sort of stand there and we say ball and strike and everything is clear-cut, that there is no judgment in the process. I do think that that's not right, and it is especially not right at the Supreme Court level."[37] In decisions on corporate contributions to political campaigns in 2010 (discussed in Chapter Four) and the constitutionality of the Affordable Care Act in 2012, the Court was not guided by the baseball analogy.

When President Obama announced his choice of Judge Sonia Sotomayor for associate justice, he spoke about the importance "of the limits of the judicial role, an understanding that a judge's job is to interpret, not make, law." At her confirmation hearing, she included this sentence in her opening statement: "The task of a judge is not to make the law—it is to apply the law." No doubt judges have the duty to apply the law, but often that is indistinguishable from making the law. Federal courts, especially the Supreme Court, are constantly creating new rules that have the force of law.

Recess Appointments

The Senate is denied a role in the confirmation process when the president makes recess appointments, including to the Supreme Court. Under Article II, Section 2, the president

---

37. Her testimony on the baseball analogy can be watched at www
.gawker.com/5576853/elena-kagan-hopefully-kills-umpire-metaphor
-for-good. Accessed Feb. 19, 2013.

"shall have Power to fill up all Vacancies that may happen during the Recess of the Senate, by granting Commissions which may expire at the end of their next Session." During the 1950s, President Eisenhower placed three men on the Supreme Court while the Senate recessed: Earl Warren, William J. Brennan, Jr., and Potter Stewart. All three joined the Court and participated in decisions before the Senate had an opportunity to review their qualifications and consider their confirmation. In each case, the Senate later gave its advice and consent.

The experience convinced Congress that the procedure was defective, both for legislative interests and the judiciary. How could federal judges serving under a recess appointment maintain judicial independence in deciding cases? Would anticipation of questions asked during a Senate confirmation hearing influence the direction of a ruling? Would a recess appointee shade an opinion to attract White House support for a lifetime appointment?[38] Litigants are entitled to have their cases heard and decided by federal judges with full independence. They lack that confidence with recess appointees. Similar questions might be asked of lower court judges who have lifetime appointments. They could be tempted to build a record to attract White House interest in moving them to the next level. Still, the lack of judicial independence is particularly acute with recess appointees to the Supreme Court.

---

38. Scott E. Graves & Robert M. Howard, Justice Takes a Recess: Judicial Recess Appointments from George Washington to George W. Bush (2009); Steven M. Pyser, "Recess Appointments to the Federal Judiciary: An Unconstitutional Transformation of Senate Advice and Consent," 8 U. Pa. J. Const. L. 61 (2006).

Following Eisenhower's initiative, the House of Representatives expressed its concerns in a 1959 study.[39] The next year, Senator Philip A. Hart introduced a resolution to discourage this practice. It states that it is the sense of the Senate that a recess appointment to the Supreme Court "may not be wholly consistent with the best interests of the Supreme Court, the nominee who may be involved, the litigants before the Court, nor indeed the people of the United States." Such appointments should not be made "except under unusual circumstances and for the purpose of preventing or ending a demonstrable breakdown in the administration of the Court's business."[40] As a Senate resolution, it had no legally binding effect but was meant to influence executive action. The Senate labored under difficult conditions when it was asked to confirm Eisenhower's choices for a lifetime term. A negative vote would mean more than the rejection of a nominee. It would remove a sitting justice. Should senators take into account the decisions rendered during the recess appointment period? The Senate passed Hart's resolution 48 to 37, essentially along party lines. Although legally nonbinding, the Senate resolution has had an effect. No president since Eisenhower has made a recess appointment to the Supreme Court.

The president's constitutional authority to make recess appointments to a federal district court was upheld by the Second Circuit in 1962.[41] In 1983, the Ninth Circuit held

---

39. House Committee on the Judiciary, "Recess Appointments of Federal Judges," 86th Cong., 1st Sess. (Comm. Print, January 1959). See also Note, "Recess Appointments to the Supreme Court—Constitutional But Unwise?," 10 Stan. L. Rev. 124 (1957).

40. 106 Cong. Rec. 18145 (1960).

41. United States v. Allocco, 305 F.2d 704 (2d Cir. 1962), cert. denied, 371 U.S. 964 (1963).

that the president's authority under Article II could not supplant the lifetime tenure guaranteed to federal judges by Article III. A three-judge panel ruled that federal judges serving under a recess appointment lacked the independence required by the Constitution.[42] The decision by the panel was overturned by the full Ninth Circuit, sitting *en banc*. Divided seven to four, it held that there was no reason to favor the constitutional provision for lifetime appointments over the constitutional provision for recess appointments. The Ninth Circuit pointed out that presidents had made recess appointments to federal courts ever since 1789, totaling approximately 300 such appointments. The four dissenters denied the strength of that pattern, noting that with one exception (the appointment prompting this case) the federal courts had functioned since 1964 without the assistance of recess appointees.

On December 27, 2000, President Clinton selected Roger L. Gregory as a recess appointee to the Fourth Circuit. President George W. Bush submitted Gregory's name on May 9, 2001, for a lifetime appointment. The Senate approved his nomination, 93 to 1. Bush made two recess appointments to the federal courts in 2004: Charles W. Pickering for the Fifth Circuit and William H. Pryor, Jr. for the Eleventh Circuit. When Pickering's recess appointment expired, he announced he would not seek a lifetime appointment.

The fact that courts sanction the use of judicial recess appointments does not mean the elected branches are required to tolerate the practice. The decision of the Ninth Circuit in 1985 operates like an advisory opinion: recess appointments to the courts are constitutional if the elected branches agree

---

42. United States v. Woodley, 726 F.2d 1328 (9th Cir. 1983).

to make them. The Senate could discourage the practice by announcing it will automatically deny confirmation to any judge who receives a recess appointment and is later nominated for a life term.

How Many Justices? Who Do They Represent?

The size of the Supreme Court fluctuated throughout the nineteenth century, keeping pace with the creation of new circuits. A seventh justice was added in 1807 to accommodate another circuit. The size increased to nine justices in 1837, reflecting the westward expansion, and to ten by 1863 with the addition of the Pacific Circuit. This tenth justice, however, was never nominated or confirmed. Three years later Congress lowered the number to seven justices, although the membership never fell below eight. The reduction is generally viewed as a slap in the face of President Andrew Johnson, depriving him of an opportunity to name his own candidates. The Radical Republicans feared that Johnson's appointees would oppose the Reconstruction policy, which placed Southern states under closer federal control.[43] Legislation in 1869 brought the Court back up to nine justices, where it has remained ever since.

We generally associate representation with Congress, but it applies to the Supreme Court as well. Initially, representation was geographic. There was a conscious effort to assure that justices came from a variety of states to represent the people's interests. It would have been politically unacceptable for the larger states, such as New York and Virginia, to

---

43. S. Rept. No. 711, 75th Cong., 1st Sess. 13 (1937).

dominate the Court. In the early years, when the country was entirely on the Eastern seaboard, representation resulted in a balance of justices from north to south. As the nation moved westward, though, representation was needed for new states and territories. The search for territorial representation has long since disappeared. It is not unusual to have two justices from a small state. William Rehnquist and Sandra Day O'Connor of Arizona served on the Court at the same time. Currently, five justices are from either New York City (Ruth Bader Ginsburg, Antonin Scalia, Sonia Sotomayor, and Elena Kagan) or New Jersey (Samuel Alito).

The goal of representation next moved to religious affiliation. With the growth of the Catholic population in America, it was no longer acceptable to have only Protestants on the Court. Eventually there appeared a Catholic seat. In time, beginning with Louis Brandeis in 1916, a Jewish seat emerged. A second Jew, Benjamin Cardozo, joined the Court in 1932. His seat was filled by three successive Jews: Felix Frankfurter, Arthur Goldberg, and Abe Fortas. That line stopped when Fortas was replaced by Harry Blackmun. The Brandeis seat was also filled by a non-Jew, William Douglas.

Representation for blacks became an important issue when President Johnson nominated Thurgood Marshall to the Court in 1967. He was replaced by Clarence Thomas in 1991. The first Italian justice, Antonin Scalia, was confirmed in 1986. A second Italian, Samuel Alito, joined the Court in 2006. Three years later, the first Latino justice—Sonia Sotomayor—was sworn in. By 2012, the Court's structure had a quite "unbalanced" representation. Not only were there five justices from the New York area, but six were Catholic (Roberts, Scalia, Kennedy, Thomas, Alito, and Sotomayor) and three were Jewish (Ginsburg, Breyer, and Kagan).

In years past, justices received their law degrees from schools around the country. That type of representation has disappeared. In the current Court, all the justices received law degrees from Ivy League schools in the Northeast. Five have law degrees from Harvard (Roberts, Scalia, Kennedy, Breyer, and Kagan). Ginsburg attended Harvard Law School but received her law degree from Columbia University. Three justices graduated from Yale Law School (Thomas, Alito, and Sotomayor).[44]

How Are Cases Brought before the Court?

For appellate cases, the Court receives petitions for *certiorari*. By "granting cert" the Court calls up the records of a lower court. That decision is wholly discretionary. In addition, petitions for review are submitted by indigents, including prison inmates, sometimes in the form of handwritten notes. These requests, called *in forma pauperis* (in the manner of a pauper), number in the thousands each term. Finally, an appellate court may submit a writ of certification to seek instruction on a question of law. This procedure is seldom used because it forces the Court to decide questions of law without the guidance of findings and conclusions from lower courts. Out of all these petitions, the Court issues fewer than 80 signed opinions a year, down from 164 opinions in the 1986–87 term.[45] Additionally, three or four decisions a year are disposed of by a brief *per curiam* opinion that announces the Court's judgment on an issue without a signed and fully developed argument.

---

44. Lawrence Baum, The Supreme Court 52–53 (10th ed., 2010).
45. Fisher & Harriger, *supra* note 6, at 162.

After a case is accepted by the Court, it is transferred to the oral argument list. In preparation for oral argument, counsel for each side submit briefs and records that are distributed to each justice. The Court schedules oral argument in public session to listen to cases, usually devoting an hour to each case. Oral argument allows justices to explore with counsel certain issues not adequately developed in the briefs. During oral argument, the chief justice sits in the center of a raised bench with the senior associate justice to his right and the next-ranking justice to his left. Other justices are arrayed by seniority alternately to his right and left, leaving the most junior justice positioned farthest to his left. Some justices rely on a bench memorandum prepared by their law clerks to digest the facts and arguments of both sides and provide guidance for the questioning of counsel.

The justices meet regularly in a conference room to discuss and vote on a number of issues. To preserve confidentiality in the conference room, only the justices are present. The chief justice begins the discussion of each case. He summarizes the facts, analyzes the law, and announces his proposed vote. He is followed by the other justices, in order of seniority. If the chief justice has voted with the majority in conference, he assigns the majority opinion either to himself or to another justice. When the chief justice is in the minority, the senior justice voting with the majority assigns the case. The dissenters decide who shall write the dissenting opinion. Each justice may write a separate opinion, concurrence, or dissent. Also in conference, the justices vote to grant or withhold cert. Four votes are needed to grant cert. There have been cases where the Court grants cert and later, on the basis of new developments, dismisses the writ of *certiorari* as "improvidently granted." Dismissing a case in this manner is sometimes called "digging a case" (*dig* standing for *dismissed as improvidently granted*).[46]

The process of writing opinions begins by reviewing briefs prepared by opposing counsel, research by law clerks and library staff, and often a number of briefs filed by *amici curiae* (friends of the court) to express the views of third parties that have particular interests in the case. They may bring to the attention of the Court certain facts not covered in the briefs submitted by the two litigants. Draft opinions are printed within the Court building and circulated among the justices. Comments are written on the drafts; memorandums are exchanged. A forceful and persuasive dissent may convince members of the majority to change their position, possibly creating a new majority from the dissenting position. Chief Justice Fred M. Vinson once remarked that an opinion circulated as a dissent "sometimes has so much in logic, reason, and authority to support it that it becomes the opinion of the Court."[47]

Chief Justice Charles Evans Hughes, who served from 1930 to 1941, "had no particular pride of authorship, and if in order to secure a vote he was forced to put in some disconnected or disjointed thoughts or sentences, in they went and let the law schools concern themselves with what they meant."[48] Political scientist Walter Murphy explained the types of bargaining that regularly occurred among the justices. It was not unusual for justices to shift back and forth on concurrences and dissents to develop accommodations within the Court.[49]

---

46. H. W. Perry, Jr., Deciding to Decide (1991).

47. 69 S.Ct. x (1949).

48. Edwin McElwain, "The Business of the Supreme Court as Conducted by Chief Justice Hughes," 63 Harv. L. Rev. 5, 19 (1949).

49. Walter F. Murphy, Elements of Judicial Strategy (1964).

The legal profession no longer seriously argues that determining whether a statute is constitutional is a mechanical process. That kind of jurisprudence was promoted by Justice Owen Roberts in 1936. He said that when an act of Congress is challenged as not conforming to the Constitution, the judiciary "has only one duty,—to lay the article of the Constitution which is invoked beside the statute which is challenged and to decide whether the latter squares with the former."[50] Nevertheless, some justices maintain they have the capacity to put aside their personal value systems. Justice Frankfurter offered this argument in 1954: "It is asked with sophomoric brightness, does a man cease to be himself when he becomes a justice? Does he change his character by putting on a gown? No, he does not change his character. He brings his whole experience, his training, his outlook, his social, intellectual and moral environment with him when he takes a seat on the Supreme Bench. But a judge worth his salt is in the grip of his function. The intellectual habits of self-discipline which govern his mind are as much a part of him as the influence of the interest he may have represented at the bar, often much more so."[51]

It would be superficial to suggest that justices use their office simply to expound on personal views. Still, decisions flow at least in part from their values and attitudes. The votes of justices cannot be predicted with mathematical accuracy, but attorneys are sufficiently alert to engage in "forum shopping" to find the court or circuit that augurs best for their client. It is now routine to recognize definite alignments and alliances among justices. After Justice Harry Blackmun

---

50. United States v. Butler, 297 U.S. 1, 62 (1936).
51. 98 Proceedings Am. Phil. Soc. 233, 238 (1954).

joined the Court in 1970, he calculated that there were two justices on the right, two on the left, and "five of us in the center."[52] Today, the Court is basically split between five conservatives and four moderate-liberals. Attorneys try to identify a particular justice they can appeal to, moving the majority in their favor.

Justices frequently complain, with good cause, that the press distorts their decisions. Misconceptions by the media are not unusual given the time pressures between the release of an opinion and the deadlines imposed by newspapers and broadcast services. However, in deciding a particular case, justices often stray from the issue being litigated and add extraneous matter in the form of *obiter dicta*—remarks that are not only collateral and incidental, but may be factually false. Justices have personal idiosyncrasies that invite affectation, ornate prose, and verbosity. Ambiguity is likely when several justices of different persuasions need to compromise to form a majority. Some of the "distortions" promoted by the press result from justices who use careless language in their opinions. When the Supreme Court announced its 1962 decision striking down a school prayer drafted by New York, a concurrence by Justice Douglas suggested that the Court's ruling would cover other ceremonial observances, such as the Court's traditional invocation when it convenes or the offering of a daily prayer by a chaplain in Congress.[53] His speculations went far beyond the particular case decided by the Court and helped fuel public confusion and outrage. Matters were not helped when the president of the American Bar Association inaccurately warned that the decision would

---

52. "A Justice Speaks Out: A Conversation with Harry A. Blackmun," Cable News Network, Inc., November 25, 1982, at 22.

53. Engel v. Vitale, 370 U.S. 421, 439–42 (1962).

require the elimination of "In God We Trust" from all coins.[54] Not only does *obiter dicta* confuse the media and the public; it also creates substantial doubts in the lower courts, executive agencies, and U.S. attorneys who must try to implement the amorphous policy announced by the Court.

Coherence and principled decision-making are difficult goals for a multimember Court that operates as a committee, attempting to stitch together decisions that can attract a majority. Efforts by 535 members of Congress to reach agreement on a bill are clearly difficult. Is should be easier for five of nine justices to issue a more intelligible decision. However, as noted by one Fourth Amendment scholar, the Court "is in the unenviable posture of a committee attempting to draft a horse by placing very short lines on a very large drawing-board at irregular intervals during which the committee constantly changes."[55]

Chief Justice Warren believed law could be distinguished from politics. Progress in politics, he said, "could be made and most often was made by compromising and taking half a loaf where a whole loaf could not be obtained." He insisted that the "opposite is true so far as the judicial process [is] concerned." Through the judicial process "and particularly in the Supreme Court, the basic ingredient of decision is principle, and it should not be compromised and parceled out a little in one case, a little more in another, until eventually someone receives the full benefit."[56] That view was published in 1977. Surely he could have recalled the obvious "compromise" in

---

54. Chester A. Newland, "Press Coverage of the United States Supreme Court," 17 West. Pol. Q. 15, 28 (1964).

55. Anthony G. Amsterdam, "Perspectives on the Fourth Amendment," 58 Minn. L. Rev. 349, 350 (1974).

56. Earl Warren, The Memoirs of Earl Warren 6 (1977).

the first desegregation decision in 1954, where the Court pretended to have a unanimous front only because it planned to issue a decision a year later explaining that desegregation could proceed with "all deliberate speed," signaling to the Southern states that they could take their sweet time in moving toward integrated public schools. Details on the two desegregation cases are covered at the end of Chapter Five.

The judicial process turns out to be quite piecemeal, and for good reason. The Supreme Court prefers to avoid general rules that exceed the necessities of a particular case. Especially in the realm of constitutional law, it recognizes the "embarrassment which is likely to result from an attempt to formulate rules or decide questions beyond the necessities of the immediate issue." The Court prefers to follow a "gradual approach to the general by a systematically guarded application and extension of constitutional principles to particular cases as they arise, rather than by out of hand attempts to establish general rules to which future cases must be fitted."[57] At times the Court has decided to speak in broad terms, opening itself to likely errors of interpretation. Many of those decisions are analyzed in this book.

Chief Justice Warren's attempt to distinguish the judicial process cleanly from the process followed by the elected branches is an illusion. Compromise, expediency, and ad hoc actions are no less a part of the process by which a multimember Court gropes incrementally toward a consensus and decision. After he left the Court, Justice Potter Stewart reflected on the decision to exclude from the courtroom evidence that had been illegally seized. He described a process that was tentative, makeshift, and improvised (See Box 2.3).

---

57. Euclid v. Ambler Co., 272 U.S. 365, 397 (1926).

> **Box 2.3**
>
> **Justice Stewart on Ad-Hoc Decisions**
>
> Looking back, the exclusionary rule seems a bit jerry-built—like a roller coaster track constructed while the roller coaster sped along. Each new piece of track was attached hastily and imperfectly to the one before it, just in time to prevent the roller coaster from crashing, but without an opportunity to measure the curves and dips preceding it or to contemplate the twists and turns that inevitably lay ahead. With the wisdom of hindsight, it is certainly possible to criticize opinions dealing with the exclusionary rule for misapplying or misconstruing prior precedents and for failing to consider how any given decision would affect the future development of the law.
>
> *Source:* Potter Stewart, "The Road to Mapp v. Ohio and Beyond: The Origins, Development and Future of the Exclusionary Rule in Search-and-Seizure Cases," 83 Colum. L. Rev. 1365, 1366 (1983).

A Variety of Voices

At the urging of colleagues who fear that dissents will damage the corporate image of the Supreme Court, justices have been willing to convert a dissent into a concurring opinion. However, it is not unusual for a concurrence to shred the logic, reasoning, and precedents promoted by the majority opinion.[58] Justices may also withhold dissents when a case is of minimal significance to them. Their actions can promote

---

58. Murphy v. Waterfront Comm'n, 378 U.S. 52, 80–92 (1964) (Harlan, J., concurring); Warden v. Hayden, 387 U.S. 294, 310–12 (1967) (Fortas, J. and Warren, C.J., concurring); Argersinger v. Hamlin, 407 U.S. 215, 41–44 (1972) (Burger, C.J., concurring) and 44–46 (Powell, J. concurring, joined by Rehnquist, J.).

institutional harmony and permit the acquiescent justices to ask a colleague for reciprocal favors.[59]

Constitutional cases may spawn a number of concurring and dissenting opinions. Justice Rehnquist suggested it "may well be that the nature of constitutional adjudication invites, at least, if it does not require, more separate opinions than does adjudication of issues of law in other areas."[60] Of special concern is the Court's inability to prepare a decision that attracts a majority of justices. Instead, the Court delivers a plurality opinion of three or four justices, which creates confusion in the lower courts and the other branches of government. The number of plurality opinions by the Warren Burger Court exceeded the number of all previous Courts.[61]

In 1977, the Supreme Court announced a rule for determining the meaning of a plurality holding. Borrowing language from *Gregg* v. *Georgia* (1976), it stated: "When a fragmented Court decides a case and no single rationale explaining the result enjoys the assent of five justices, 'the holding of the Court may be viewed as that position taken by those Members who concurred in the judgments on the narrowest grounds.'"[62] One study concluded that this guidance was "insupportable and should be rejected."[63]

---

59. Walter F. Murphy, Elements of Judicial Strategy 52–53 (1964).

60. William H. Rehnquist, "The Supreme Court: Past and Present," 59 A.B.A.J. 361, 363 (1973).

61. Note, "Plurality Decisions and Judicial Decisionmaking." 94 Harv. L. Rev. 1127 (1981); John F. Davis & William L. Reynolds, "Juridical Cripples: Plurality Opinions in the Supreme Court," 1974 Duke L. J. 59 (1974).

62. Marks v. United States, 430 U.S. 188, 193 (1977).

63. Mark Alan Thurmond, "When the Court Divides: Reconsidering the Precedential Value of Supreme Court Plurality Decisions," 42 Duke L. J. 419, 421 (1992).

Shortly before returning to the Supreme Court—this time as chief justice—in 1930 after his 1916 resignation, Charles Evans Hughes acknowledged that a dissenting opinion may damage the appearance of justice and certainty that the public expects from the Court. However, he felt it far more injurious to announce an artificial and deceptive consensus. A unanimous opinion "which is merely formal, which is recorded at the expense of strong, conflicting views, is not desirable in a court of last resort, whatever may be the effect upon public opinion at the time." What builds public confidence in the Court is its "character and independence." A dissent by a justice "is an appeal to the brooding spirit of the law, to the intelligence of a future day, when a later decision may possibly correct the error into which the dissenting judge believes the court to have been betrayed."[64] Justice Douglas added: "Certainty and unanimity in the law are possible both under the fascist and communist systems. They are not only possible, they are indispensable."[65]

An example of a dissent that appealed to the "brooding spirit of the law" was written by Justice John Marshall Harlan in the *Civil Rights Cases* (1883). Congress passed legislation in 1875 to give freed blacks equal access to public accommodations, including inns, theaters, and public transportation.[66] Eight years later the Court struck down the law as a federal encroachment on the states and an interference with private relationships. Justice Harlan penned the sole dissent, pointing out with careful analysis why the majority's opinion was

---

64. Charles Evans Hughes, The Supreme Court of the United States 67–68 (1928).

65. William O. Douglas, "The Dissent: A Safeguard of Democracy," 32 J. Am. Judicature Society 104, 104 (December 1948).

66. 18 Stat. 335 (1875).

narrow and artificial, and offering detailed facts and precedents to support the congressional judgment. His painstaking analysis eventually became the nation's policy, but not until the 1960s, after costly years of the Court embracing judicial supremacy as the highest possible value.[67] This case from 1883 is explored in Chapter Five.

In an article published in 1955, Justice Robert H. Jackson cautioned about the motivation and reliability of some dissents. The preparation of the majority opinion is necessarily restricted by the need to attract five justices, or at least a plurality. There is no such limit on the dissenter. Justice Jackson refuted the idea that dissenting opinions clarify the issues: "Often they do the exact opposite. The technique of the dissenter often is to exaggerate the holding of the Court beyond the meaning of the majority and then to blast away at the excess." To Jackson, "there is nothing good, for either the Court or the dissenter, in dissenting per se."[68]

---

67. Louis Fisher, Defending Congress and the Constitution 111–20 (2011).

68. Robert H. Jackson, The Supreme Court in the American System of Government 18–19 (1955).

Chapter Three
"Self-Inflicted Wounds"

This book's preface includes a remark by Justice Robert H. Jackson: "We are not final because we are infallible, but we are infallible only because we are final."[1] The flippant, superficial quality of his sentence is surprising, coming from someone who over the years demonstrated unusual sophistication in understanding the Supreme Court's role in democratic government. The Court has been neither infallible nor final. Why resort to a strained, erroneous claim? The Court can comfortably point to many decisions that strengthened the country, including checks on presidential war power, reapportionment, the rights of defendants, protecting a free press, and the Watergate Tapes Case.[2]

This chapter reviews some decisions that damaged both the Court and the nation. Perhaps by acknowledging the Court's capacity to make errors in the past, justices might

---

1. Brown v. Allen, 344 U.S. 443, 540 (1953).

2. Youngstown Co. v. Sawyer, 343 U.S. 579 (1952) (striking down President Truman's seizure of steel mills); Baker v. Carr, 369 U.S. 186 (1962) (declaring malapportionment a violation of equal protection); Gideon v. Wainwright, 372 U.S. 335 (1963) (entitling indigent defendants to assistance of counsel); New York Times Co. v. Sullivan, 376 U.S.

make fewer in the future. Even if that objective is not attained, it is important for scholars, the media, and the public to keep in mind the times the Court fell short in protecting the law, the Constitution, and individual rights. With less adulation and fawning from the outside, justices might be more circumspect and decide cases better grounded in law and institutional judgment.

Three Selections by a Chief Justice

Chief Justice Charles Evans Hughes published a book, based on lectures delivered in 1927, that generally praises the Supreme Court while recognizing that it "has the inevitable failings of any human institution." He remarked: "You can find in imperfect human beings, for the essential administration of justice, a rectitude of purpose, a clarity of vision and a capacity for independence and balanced judgment."[3] Still, Hughes acknowledged that "in three noticeable instances the Court has suffered from self-inflicted wounds."[4] He offered these examples: *Dred Scott* v. *Sandford* in 1857, the *Legal Tender Cases* in 1870–71, and the *Income Tax Cases* in 1895. His list is only a starting point. Judicial

---

254 (1964) (protecting newspapers from libel suits); and United States v. Nixon, 418 U.S. 683 (1974) (forcing President Nixon to release the Watergate tapes). Some might add *Brown* v. *Board of Education* (1954) and *Roe* v. *Wade* (1973), but the first is a complex story treated in Chapter Five. I regard the abortion decision as a serious misjudgment in terms of the trimester framework and cover it in Chapter Four.

    3. Charles Evans Hughes, The Supreme Court of the United States 45–46 (1936).

    4. Id. at 50.

errors in addition to those selected by Hughes are identified in this and other chapters.

1. Dred Scott. In this case, the Court considered two principal issues. First: Could a black man sue in federal court? Second: Did Congress possess authority to prohibit slavery in the territories? James Buchanan, newly elected president, decided to entrust those concerns solely to the Court. In his inaugural address on March 4, 1857, he regarded the issues as presenting "a judicial question, which legitimately belongs to the Supreme Court of the United States, before whom it is now pending, and will, it is understood, be speedily and finally settled. To their decision, in common with all good citizens, I shall cheerfully submit, whatever this may be."[5]

Buchanan received advance knowledge from several justices about the content of the draft ruling and its near completion. The decision was indeed speedy. The Court released its opinion two days after the inaugural address. Writing for the Court, Chief Justice Roger Taney held that Dred Scott, as a black man, was not a citizen of Missouri within the meaning of the Constitution and was not entitled to sue in federal court. In Taney's words: "The only matter in issue before the court, therefore, is whether the descendants of such slaves, when they shall be emancipated, or who are born of parents who had become free before their birth, are citizens of a State, in the sense in which the word citizen is used in the Constitution of the United States."[6]

---

5. Arthur M. Schlesinger, Jr. and Fred L. Israel, eds., My Fellow Citizens: The Inaugural Addresses of the Presidents of the United States, 1789–2009, at 132 (2010).

6. 60 U.S. (19 How.) 393, 403 (1857).

For Taney the answer was clear. He considered blacks "a subordinate and inferior class of beings, who had been subjugated by the dominant race, and, whether emancipated or not, yet remained subject to their authority, and had no rights or privileges but such as those who held the power and the Government might choose to grant them."[7] Moreover, Congress had no constitutional authority to prohibit slavery in the territories.[8] To Taney, the Constitution recognized "the right of property of the master in a slave" and made "no distinction between that description of property and other property owned by a citizen."[9]

Although President Buchanan accurately predicted that the Court's ruling would be speedy, he was incorrect that a judicial decision would render the slavery issue "finally settled." The Court's decision helped precipitate a civil war that left, out of a population of 30 million, more than 600,000 dead and 400,000 wounded. To Chief Justice Hughes, even assuming "the sincerity of the judges who took this view, the grave injury that the Court sustained through its action has been universally recognized. Its action was a public calamity."[10]

Dred Scott was formally overturned by the Fourteenth Amendment, ratified in 1868, but it was politically repudiated long before that. In his inaugural address in 1861, Abraham Lincoln denied that constitutional questions could be settled solely by the Supreme Court. If government policy on "vital questions affecting the whole people is to be irrevocably

---

7. Id. at 404–05.

8. Id. at 447–52.

9. Id. at 451.

10. Hughes, *supra* note 3, at 50.

fixed" by the Court, "the people will have ceased to be their own rulers."[11] In legislation enacted in 1862, Congress asserted its independent constitutional authority by prohibiting slavery in the territories, with or without the Court's imprimatur.[12] In that same year, Attorney General Edward Bates released a legal opinion that shredded the rest of *Dred Scott*. He concluded that men of color, if born in America, are citizens of the United States.[13]

2. Legal Tender Cases.   Hughes explained that in the years following *Dred Scott* the Court "was still suffering from lack of a satisfactory measure of public confidence." Yet it chose, with the *Legal Tender Cases* in 1870–71, to act in a manner that once again "brought the Court into disesteem."[14] In 1866, Congress reduced the number of justices "in order to deprive [Democratic] President [Andrew] Johnson of the opportunity to make appointments."[15] After Republican Ulysses S. Grant became president, the number of justices was increased to nine. There were two vacancies on the Court when the first legal tender case, *Hepburn* v. *Griswold,* was decided. It involved a statute passed by Congress during the Civil War, treating paper money as legal tender for discharging prior debts. With a bench of seven justices and three in dissent, the Court held that the money ("greenbacks") was unconstitutional. The four justices in the majority were Democrats; the three dissenters were Republicans. In the lower federal courts, almost every

---

11. 7 A Compilation of the Messages and Papers of the Presidents 3210 (James D. Richardson, ed.). Hereafter "Richardson."

12. 12 Stat. 432 (1862).

13. 10 Op. Att'y Gen. 382 (1862).

14. Hughes, *supra* note 3, at 51.

Democratic judge declared the statute unconstitutional; nearly every Republican judge sustained it.[16]

The retirement of Justice Robert Grier and the congressional authorization the previous year of a new justice allowed President Grant to appoint two new members. He had reason to believe that both choices would support the Legal Tender Act. William Strong, as a member of the Supreme Court of Pennsylvania, had already sustained the statute. Grant's second choice, Joseph P. Bradley, appeared to be no less sympathetic. Fifteen months after the Legal Tender Act had been declared unconstitutional, a reconstituted Court upheld it 5–4. Strong and Bradley joined the original three dissenters to form the majority.[17] Chief Justice Hughes concluded: "From the standpoint of the effect on public opinion, there can be no doubt that the reopening of the case was a serious mistake and the overruling in such a short time, and by one vote, of the previous decision shook popular respect for the Court."[18] The second decision laid bare that a constitutional decision depends not solely on conscientious, objective interpretation by justices, trained in the law, but on who sits on the Court.

3. Income Tax Cases. Hughes's final example of a judicial self-inflicted wound is two decisions in 1895 on the taxing power. In his words, "Twenty-five years later [after the *Legal Tender Cases*], when the Court had recovered its prestige,

---

15. Id.

16. Charles Fairman, "Mr. Justice Bradley's Appointment to the Supreme Court and the Legal Tender Cases," 54 Harv. L. Rev. 1128, 1131 (1941).

17. Legal Tender Cases, 12 Wall. (79 U.S.) 457 (1871).

18. Hughes, *supra* note 3, at 52.

its action in the income tax cases gave occasion for a bitter assault."[19] A unanimous Court in 1881 had upheld a federal income tax passed in 1864 to finance the Civil War. It did so by calling it an indirect tax, concluding that direct taxes (requiring apportionment under Article I, Section 9) "are only capitation taxes ... and taxes on real estates."[20] Capitation taxes are also called "head taxes" (applied to each person).

In 1895, however, the Court struck down a federal income tax, treating it as a direct tax to be apportioned on the basis of population. In the first of two decisions, the Court held that a tax on rents or income of real estate was a direct tax and violated the Constitution by not being apportioned.[21] On the question of whether the income tax was a direct or indirect tax, the justices were evenly divided, 4 to 4.[22] The Court acted under the shadow of class warfare and threats of socialism. During oral argument, attorney Joseph H. Choate warned the justices that the income tax was "communistic in its purposes and tendencies, and is defended here upon principles as communistic, socialistic—what shall I call them—populistic as ever have been addressed to any political assembly in the world."[23]

Upon rehearing, a 5–4 decision invalidated the income tax, treating it as a direct tax to be apportioned on the basis of population.[24] Justice Howell Edmunds Jackson, who did not participate in the first decision because of illness, voted in

---

19. Id. at 53.

20. Springer v. United States, 102 U.S. 586, 602 (1881).

21. Pollock v. Farmers' Loan & Trust Co., 157 U.S. 429, 583 (1895).

22. Id. at 586.

23. Id. at 532.

24. Pollock v. Farmers' Loan & Trust Co., 158 U.S. 601, 537 (1895).

favor of the income tax in the second case.[25] All things being equal, that should have produced a 5–4 majority *upholding* the income tax. However, another justice switched his vote to build a majority against the income tax. Who he was, and why he switched, was not disclosed.[26] This kind of razor-thin majority and sudden vote-switching undermined the reputation of the Court. Not until 1913 did Congress and the states pass the Sixteenth Amendment to override the Court.

Three other decisions by the Supreme Court during the nineteenth century (though not noted by Chief Justice Hughes) damaged the Court's reputation as guardian of individual rights: **(4.)** *Bradwell* v. *State* (1873), involving the right of women to practice law; **(5.)** the *Civil Rights Cases* of 1883, striking down a congressional statute that provided blacks with equal accommodation to public facilities; and **(6.)** *Plessy* v. *Ferguson* (1896), upholding the "separate but equal" doctrine for blacks in railroad cars. Those three are analyzed in Chapter Five.

Checks on Judicial Finality

Before turning to judicial decisions in the twentieth century, it is helpful to review a number of cases from 1789 to 1895 that underscore why Supreme Court decisions on constitutional matters are not necessarily final. Early on, justices were astounded when the Court's constitutional decisions were reversed by the elected branches. In time, the Court learned that it was only one voice in determining the meaning of the

---

25. Hughes, *supra* note 3, at 54.
26. Id.

Constitution. That task would be shared with Congress, the president, and often the general public.

7. McCulloch. In 1819, the Supreme Court upheld the constitutionality of the U.S. Bank.[27] As author of *McCulloch* v. *Maryland,* Chief Justice Marshall seemed to promote the doctrine of judicial supremacy. He said that if a constitutional dispute must be decided, "by this tribunal alone can the decision be made. On the supreme court of the United States has the constitution of our country devolved this important duty."[28]

That was incorrect. At stake in this U.S. Bank case was whether the two elected branches wanted to create such an institution. It was at their discretion to create it or not. Even if the Court were to bless their efforts, a future Congress or future president could make an independent decision on a national bank. If Congress were to decide not to reauthorize it, the political decision would be closed and final. The Court had no part. If Congress were to reauthorize the bank and the president vetoed it on policy or constitutional grounds, the bank would again be invalidated unless Congress could muster votes to override the veto. Those decisions by the elected branches on a national bank could not be second-guessed by the Court. *McCulloch* has been described as one of the "fixed stars in our constitutional constellation."[29] No one should doubt its importance, but it has nothing to do with judicial finality.

---

27. McCulloch v. Maryland, 17 U.S. (4 Wheat.) 316 (1819).

28. Id. at 401.

29. Jamal Greene, "The Anticanon," 125 Harv. L. Rev. 379, 385 (2011).

Consider what happened in 1832 when Congress chose to reauthorize the bank. President Andrew Jackson was urged to sign the bill because the bank had been endorsed by previous Congresses, previous presidents, and the Supreme Court. Supposedly he was duty-bound to sign the bill. In issuing a veto, Jackson rejected that advice. He considered "mere precedent" a "dangerous source of authority ... [that] should not be regarded as deciding questions of constitutional power except where the acquiescence of the people and the States can be considered as well settled."[30] He reviewed the checkered history of the bank. The elected branches favored a national bank in 1791, decided against it in 1811 and 1815, and returned their support in 1816. At the state level, legislative, executive, and judicial opinions on the constitutionality of the bank were mixed. Jackson found nothing in this record persuasive or decisive. Congress sustained his veto.

To Jackson, even if Chief Justice Marshall's opinion on the bank in 1819 "covered the whole ground of this act, it ought not to control the coordinate authorities of this Government." All three branches, he said, "must each for itself be guided by its own opinion of the Constitution." Each public official takes an oath to support the Constitution "as he understands it, and not as it is understood by others." His veto message, which Congress sustained, articulated the theory of coordinate construction—a process involving all three branches of government (see Box 3.1).

8. The Wheeling Bridge Cases. Judicial and congressional actions in the 1850s again demonstrate why the Supreme Court need not have the final word on constitutional issues. In 1852, the Court decided that the Wheeling Bridge over the

---

30. 3 Richardson 1144–45.

Box 3.1

Jackson's Veto Message

It is as much the duty of the House of Representatives, of the Senate, and of the President to decide upon the constitutionality of any bill or resolution which may be presented to them for passage or approval as it is of the supreme judges when it may be brought before them for judicial decision. The opinion of the judges has no more authority over Congress than the opinion of Congress has over the judges, and on that point the President is independent of both. The authority of the Supreme Court must not, therefore, be permitted to control the Congress or the Executive when acting in their legislative capacities, but to have only such influence as the force of their reasoning may deserve.

Source: 3 Messages and Papers of the Presidents 1145 (Richardson, ed.).

Ohio River, constructed under Virginia state law, constituted a nuisance because the structure was so low it obstructed navigation.[31] The Court appointed a commissioner to determine the facts about the bridge. By measuring its height, the water level, and the height of the chimneys on approaching boats, he concluded that the bridge represented an obstruction over a navigable stream. Final word on a constitutional issue? Not at all.

The Court released its decision on February 6, 1852, and in amended form in May. On August 12 the House of Representatives debated a bill to make the Wheeling Bridge "a lawful structure."[32] A sponsor of this legislation insisted that the "ultimate right" to decide the issue "was in

---

31. Pennsylvania v. Wheeling and Belmont Bridge Co., 54 U.S. (13 How.) 518 (1852).

32. Cong. Globe, 32d Cong., 1st Sess. 2195 (1852).

Congress" pursuant to its power to regulate interstate commerce and preserve the intercourse between states.[33] Other lawmakers regarded the bill as constitutionally improper. Asked Representative Carlton B. Curtis: "Should Congress sit as a court of errors and appeals over the decision and adjudication of the Supreme Court of the United States, and consider matters which, without a doubt, properly belonged to that tribunal, and review them in a manner entirely unknown to law?"[34]

Was the dispute, however, one of law or fact? If the latter, the fact-finding capacity of the legislative branch was certainly equal to, if not superior to, that of the judiciary. The Court had decided to shift the investigation to a commissioner. Why should his judgment transcend that of Congress? Senator George Edmund Badger denied that Congress was seeking "some revising power over the adjudications of the Supreme Court." Instead, Congress was exercising "our legislative functions, as the court discharged its judicial function." The bill required vessels navigating the Ohio River "to conform the elevation of their chimneys to the height of the bridge, in the exercise of our undoubted right to regulate and control the commerce of the river."[35] Rather than altering the bridge to accommodate vessels, ships should adjust to the bridge. To Badger, it was a "question of expediency" best left to the legislative branch: "Shall seven steamboats, out of the three hundred and fifty navigating the Ohio, be

---

33. Id. at 2195 (Rep. Joseph Addison Woodward).

34. Id. at 2240. Curtiss's full speech appears at 967–68. Other speeches on the Wheeling Bridge appear at 967–68, 972–74, 974–77, 1037–41, 1041–44, 1044–47, 1047–49, 1065–68, 1068–71.

35. Id. at 2310.

put to the trouble of reducing their smoke-pipes five or six feet, so as to be able to pass under the bridge?"[36]

Other lawmakers pointed out that the legal dispute was deliberately provoked by Pittsburgh steamboats that elevated their smoke chimneys so they could not clear the bridge.[37] The issue was not purely legal or constitutional; it was in large part one of fact. Senator Walker Brooke remarked: "In all legal questions, I am willing, and more than willing, to yield to the authority of the Supreme Court; but, in questions of fact, I conceive, that, as a member of the Congress of the United States, I have the same right of judgment, humble as I am, as the Supreme Court has." In view of evidence that steamboats had intentionally elevated their chimneys "to an unnecessary height, for the purpose of destroying the structure," Brooke said he would do "everything I can, as a legislator, to nullify, if I may use the expression, the decision of the Supreme Court."[38]

Legislative language on the Wheeling Bridge was placed in an appropriations bill enacted on August 31, 1852, three months after the Court's amended decision. Section 6 of the bill provided: "*And be it further enacted,* That the bridges across the Ohio River at Wheeling, in the State of Virginia, and at Bridgeport, in the State of Ohio, abutting on Zane's Island, in said river, are hereby declared to be lawful structures in their present position and elevation, and shall be so held and taken to be, any thing in any law or laws of the United States to the contrary notwithstanding." Section 7 authorized the Wheeling and Belmont Bridge Company to "have and

---

36. Id. at 2440.

37. Id. (Senator James Murray Mason).

38. Id.

maintain their said bridges at their present site and elevation" and required vessels navigating the Ohio River to ensure that any pipes and chimneys shall not "interfere with the elevation and construction of said bridges."[39]

The dispute returned to the Supreme Court when Pennsylvania insisted that the congressional statute was "unconstitutional and void."[40] Writing for the majority, Justice Samuel Nelson explained that in 1852 the Court regarded the bridge as inconsistent with the authority of Congress to regulate interstate commerce. The new statute removed that objection.[41] What of the argument that Congress lacked authority to annul a court's judgment already rendered? As a general rule, Nelson agreed that Congress could not annul "adjudication upon the private rights of parties," but he distinguished the Wheeling case from that category. Because of the new statute, he determined, "the bridge is no longer an unlawful obstruction" and "it is quite plain the decree of the court cannot be enforced."[42]

Three dissenters were aghast. Justice John McLean objected: "It was said by Chief Justice Marshall, many years ago, that congress could do many things, but that it would not alter a fact. This it has attempted to do in the above act."[43] Was McLean arguing that the Court could alter a fact but Congress could not? He concluded that the new statute, "being the exercise of a judicial and appellate power," was

---

39. 10 Stat. 112 (1852).

40. Pennsylvania v. Wheeling and Belmont Bridge Co., 18 How. 421, 429 (1856).

41. Id. at 430.

42. Id. at 432.

43. Id. at 439.

unconstitutional.[44] Of course, members of Congress regarded their action as the exercise of legislative, not judicial, power. Justice Robert Grier, in another dissent, declared that allowing Congress to annul or vacate a Supreme Court decree "is without precedent, and, as a precedent for the future, it is of dangerous example."[45] Precedents did exist, however. If Chief Justice Marshall in *McCulloch* decided that the U.S. Bank was constitutional, nothing prevented Congress and the president in future years from deciding that the bank lacked constitutional legitimacy. A third dissent came from Justice James Wayne: "Whatever congress may have intended by the act of August, 1852, I do not think it admits of the interpretation given to it by the majority of the court; and if it does, then my opinion is that the act would be unconstitutional."[46]

The position of these three dissenters did not prevail. No clear line separates what is legislative (the domain of Congress) and what is judicial (the domain of the courts). States lacking authority over interstate commerce at one point can have their powers strengthened by an act of Congress. As the Court noted in 1946: "Whenever Congress' judgment has been uttered affirmatively to contradict the Court's previously expressed view that specific action taken by the states in Congress' silence was forbidden by the commerce clause, this body has accommodated its previous judgment to Congress' expressed approval."[47] In 1985, the Court said that when Congress "so chooses, state actions which it plainly authorizes are invulnerable to constitutional attack under

---

44. Id. at 443.

45. Id. at 449.

46. Id. at 450.

47. Prudential Ins. Co. v. Benjamin, 328 U.S. 408, 425 (1946).

the Commerce Clause."[48] In a concurrence in 1995, Justices Anthony Kennedy and Sandra Day O'Connor conceded that "if we invalidate a state law, Congress can in effect overturn our judgment."[49]

9. Regulating Intoxicating Liquors. This type of dialogue between Congress and the Court is not unusual. In other areas of constitutional law, after the Court determines that a state lacks authority to regulate an economic activity, it may reverse itself when Congress enters the picture to enact legislation that supports the state. In 1890, the Court ruled that a state's prohibition of intoxicating liquors from outside its borders could not be applied to original packages or kegs. A firm in Illinois transported sealed kegs of beer to Keokuk, Iowa, where a state official seized the property and took it into custody because Iowa prohibited the sale of intoxicating liquors. The Court held that only after the original package entered Iowa and was broken into smaller packages could the state regulate the product. The Court added a caveat: the power of Congress over interstate commerce necessarily trumped the power of a state "unless placed there by congressional act."[50] States could not exclude incoming articles "without congressional permission."[51]

The final word on this constitutional question, therefore, belonged to Congress. The Court's opinion in *Leisy* v. *Hardin* was issued on April 28, 1890. By May 14, the Senate reported a bill to grant Iowa authority to regulate incoming

---

48. Northeast Bancorp v. Board of Governors, FRS, 472 U.S. 159, 174 (1985).

49. United States v. Lopez, 514 U.S. 549, 580 (1995).

50. Leisy v. Hardin, 155 U.S. 100, 108 (1890).

51. Id. at 125.

intoxicating liquors.[52] Imaginative entrepreneurs responded to the Court's decision by opening up "original-package saloons" to block the state from exercising any control. Brewers and distillers from outside the state began packaging their goods "even in the shape of a vial containing a single drink."[53] Congressional debate demonstrated the limitations of abstract Court doctrines ("original package") that proved unworkable in practice.

Lawmakers made a number of irreverent remarks about the Court's effort to rule in this area. Senator George Edmunds described the Court as "an independent and co-ordinate branch of the Government" empowered to decide cases, but "as it regards the Congress of the United States, its opinions are of no more value to us than ours are to it. We are just as independent of the Supreme Court of the United States as it is of us, and every judge will admit it." If members of Congress concluded that the Court made an error with its constitutional reasoning, "are we to stop and say that is the end of the law and the mission of civilization in the United States for that reason? I take it not." Courts had a record of deciding things one way and then another. Edmunds added: "As they have often done, it may be their mission next year to change their opinion and say that the rule ought to be the other way."[54]

Congress enacted remedial legislation on August 6, 1890, slightly more than three months after the Court's decision. The statute made intoxicating liquors, upon their arrival in a state or territory, subject to the police powers of a state "to the

---

52. 21 Cong. Rec. 4642 (1890).

53. Id. at 4954.

54. Id. at 4964.

same extent and in the same manner as though such liquids or liquors had been produced in such State or Territory, and shall not be exempt therefrom by reason of being introduced therein in original packages or otherwise."[55] When the constitutionality of this statute was taken to the Supreme Court, it was upheld unanimously.[56]

Twentieth-Century Wounds

A recent study in the *Harvard Law Review* singles out only two twentieth-century decisions that merit being classified as part of the "anticanon"—that is, so wrongly decided they rank as judicial mistakes: *Lochner* v. *New York* (1905) and *Korematsu* v. *United States* (1944).[57] Two other decisions—these from the nineteenth century—are also identified as clear judicial failures: *Dred Scott* and the "separate but equal" doctrine announced in *Plessy* v. *Ferguson* (1896).[58] A pair of twentieth-century cases cited as poorly reasoned include the mandatory-sterilization case of *Buck* v. *Bell* (1927) and the sodomy case of *Bowers* v. *Hardwick* (1986), but they are placed well below the four cases listed above.[59]

Dred Scott was covered in this chapter along with the *Legal Tender Cases* and the *Income Tax Cases*. This chapter now turns to *Lochner, Buck* v. *Bell,* the child-labor cases from 1918 to 1941, the "sole-organ doctrine" of *United States* v.

---

55. 20 Stat. 313 (1890).

56. In re Rahrer, 140 U.S. 545 (1891).

57. Greene, *supra* note 29, at 417–27.

58. Id. at 406–17.

59. Id. at 380–81, 383, 389.

Curtiss-Wright Export Corp. of 1936, the flag-salute case of 1940, the Nazi saboteur case in 1942, and the Japanese American cases of *Hirabayashi* and *Korematsu* in 1943 and 1944. These cases are selected because they illustrate how the Court can invent a liberty-of-contract doctrine (*Lochner*), rely on false information in a contrived case to uphold a statute (the mandatory-sterilization case), use discredited theories to block regulation (the child-labor cases), misrepresent history (*Curtiss-Wright*), place national unity over religious freedom (the flag-salute case), issue a *per curiam* decision without any legal reasoning (the Nazi saboteur case), and defer to executive branch racist policy (in the two Japanese American cases). Chapter Four examines nine other defective Court decisions issued after World War II. *Plessy* and other cases are examined in Chapter Five.

10. Lochner. In *Lochner* v. *New York* (1905), the Court struck down a state law that limited bakery workers to sixty hours a week or ten hours a day. Justice Rufus Wheeler Peckham, writing for a 5–4 majority, converted the general right to make a contract into a laissez-faire doctrine. He found no "reasonable ground" to interfere with the liberty of a person to contract for as many hours of work as desired.[60] The statute seemed to him to serve no purpose in safeguarding public health or the health of the worker. Such laws he called "mere meddlesome interferences" with the rights of an individual to freely enter into contracts. In their dissent, Justices John Marshall Harlan, Edward Douglass White, and William R. Day reviewed previous holdings of the Court that interpreted the police power of states to permit government regulation

---

60. Lochner v. New York, 198 U.S. 45, 57 (1905).

over the economy. In a separate dissent, Justice Oliver Wendell Holmes, Jr. accused the majority of deciding "upon an economic theory which a large part of the country does not entertain." The Constitution, he said, is "not intended to embody a particular economic theory, whether of paternalism and the organic relation of the citizen to the state or of *laissez faire*."[61]

Future Court rulings were not wedded to *Lochner* and its so-called "equality of right" for employers and employees to enter into a contract. In 1908, it sustained Oregon's ten-hour day for women.[62] A 5–4 Court in 1917 upheld a congressional statute setting an eight-hour day for railroad workers engaged in interstate commerce.[63] In that same year, the Court supported the constitutionality of Oregon's ten-hour day for both men and women.[64] In 1923, a 5–3 Court swung back in the other direction by holding against a congressional statute that provided for minimum wages for women and children in the District of Columbia.[65]

The philosophy of *Lochner* as well as the 1923 decision survived as late as 1936, when a 5–4 Court struck down New York's minimum-wage law for women and children. "Freedom of contract," said the Court, "is the general rule and restraint the exception."[66] The 1923 decision was finally overruled in 1937, when a 5–4 Court upheld a minimum-wage

---

61. Id. at 75.
62. Muller v. Oregon, 208 U.S. 412 (1908).
63. Wilson v. New, 243 U.S. 332 (1917).
64. Bunting v. Oregon, 243 U.S. 426 (1917).
65. Adkins v. Children's Hospital, 261 U.S. 525, 560 (1923).
66. Morehead v. N.Y. ex rel. Tipaldo, 298 U.S. 587, 610–11 (1936).

law for women and minors in the state of Washington.[67] Over
a period of about four decades, the Court tried to impose a
liberty-of-contract theory at a time when economic power
had shifted from the employee to the employer. By 1941,
three conservative justices (George Sutherland, Pierce Butler, and Willis Van Devanter) had been replaced by more
moderate justices (Stanley Forman Reed, Frank Murphy,
and Hugo Black). Subsequent decisions made it clear that
policies concerning economic and social philosophy would
be shared with the elected branches, not decided exclusively
by the courts.[68]

11. Buck v. Bell. Highly damaging to the Court's reputation and the rights of individuals was *Buck* v. *Bell* (1927),
upholding mandatory sterilization. Earlier decisions by federal
courts rejected state efforts to sterilize prisoners for reasons
of eugenics. In 1914, a federal district court struck down a
law that required a vasectomy for criminals convicted twice
of a felony (even if a felony consisted of breaking an electric
globe or unfastening a strap on a harness). The court regarded
mandatory vasectomy as a cruel and unusual punishment that
"belongs to the dark ages."[69] A Nevada law on mandatory
sterilization was struck down in 1918 because it gave judges
too much discretion.[70]

---

67. West Coast Hotel Co. v. Parrish, 300 U.S. 379 (1937).

68. E.g., Ferguson v. Skrupa, 372 U.S. 726 (1963). See also Jack M.
Balkin, "'Wrong the Day It Was Decided': Lochner and Constitutional
Historicism," 85 B. U. L. Rev. 677 (2005) and Greene, *supra* note 29, at
417–22.

69. Davis v. Berry, 216 Fed. 413, 416 (S.D. Iowa 1914).

70. Mickle v. Henrichs, 262 Fed. 687 (D. Nev. 1918).

A Virginia court in 1925 upheld the state's mandatory-sterilization law as a proper use of the police power to prevent the transmission of insanity, idiocy, imbecility, epilepsy, and crime.[71] The case involved Carrie Buck, who had been placed in a state institution at age eighteen. Her mother had been committed to the same institution, and Carrie had given birth to an illegitimate child the state claimed to be of "defective mentality." By an 8–1 majority, a three-page opinion by Justice Holmes in *Buck* v. *Bell* affirmed the state law. In his now infamous words: "Three generations of imbeciles are enough."[72]

The decision is marred in several ways. As pointed out in Chapter Two, the case was wholly contrived without any adversary quality. Irving Whitehead, Carrie's attorney, was a longtime friend of the state legislators who drafted the sterilization law and served on the board of the institution in which Carrie lived. While on the board, he helped approve the sterilization of more than two dozen women. In that capacity he worked with the institution's physician, who regularly advocated sterilization and made that recommendation for Carrie.[73] As a "friendly suit" brought by two parties that agreed on the desired outcome, the Supreme Court lacked the necessary benefit of briefs and oral argument by rivals who could properly inform the Court.

Had that process been followed, the Court would have learned that school records indicated Carrie was a normal child and that she became pregnant when raped by the nephew

---

71. Buck v. Bell, 143 Va. 310 (1925).

72. Buck v. Bell, 274 U.S. 200, 207 (1927).

73. Paul A. Lombardo, "Three Generations, No Imbeciles: New Light on Buck v. Bell," 60 N.Y.U. L. Rev. 30, 33–39, 45–50 (1985).

of foster parents she lived with for fourteen years.[74] There was no evidence that Carrie or her child were feebleminded. As for Carrie's mother, there was no evidence that she was feeble-minded either.[75] Many individuals were placed in institutions without procedural safeguards, legal counsel, or valid tests to determine their mental capacity. Justice Holmes defended the state law by arguing that if the government can send men off to war to be injured and even killed, it could order the lesser penalty of mandatory sterilization of the "unfit." It would be difficult to find Court language more vile and unreasoned (see Box 3.2).

Box 3.2

Holmes's Argument for Mandatory Sterilization

We have seen more than once that the public welfare may call upon the best of citizens for their lives. It would be strange if it could not call upon those who already sap the strength of the State for these lesser sacrifices, often not felt to be such by those concerned, in order to prevent our being swamped with incompetence. It is better for all the world, if instead of waiting to execute degenerate offspring for crime, or to let them starve for their imbecility, society can prevent those who are manifestly unfit from continuing their kind. The principle that sustains compulsory vaccination is broad enough to cover cutting the Fallopian tubes. *Jacobson* v. *Massachusetts*, 197 U.S. 11. Three generations of imbeciles are enough.

Source: Buck v. Bell, 274 U.S. 200, 207 (1927).

---

74. Id. at 52, 54.

75. Stephen Jay Gould, The Flamingo's Smile: Reflections in Natural History 311–17 (1985).

The Court's decision preceded by a few years Nazi Germany's biological experiments and its extermination of millions of Jews, Poles, gypsies, and other groups as part of a plan to produce a "master race." Today, instead of sterilization being forced on the "unfit," the operation is submitted to voluntarily each year by fit adults who do not wish to have children. Although *Buck* v. *Bell* has never been explicitly overruled, its reasoning and results have been thoroughly discredited.[76] In 2002, Virginia governor Mark Warner formally apologized for the state's policy on eugenics, under which some 8,000 people were involuntarily sterilized from 1927 to 1979. Reflecting the views of the state legislature in 2002, he said the eugenics movement "was a shameful effort in which state government never should have been involved."[77] Nationwide, the practice affected an estimated 65,000 Americans, all with the blessing of the Supreme Court.

12. Child-Labor Legislation. Two other decisions that injured the Court's reputation with regard to constitutional interpretation involved congressional efforts to regulate child labor. A third decision two decades later not only upheld legislation on child labor, but publicly apologized for deficiencies in the earlier rulings. By the turn of the twentieth century, private organizations began to lobby Congress to eliminate the harsh and unhealthy conditions of child labor. Initial efforts were at the state level, until it became clear that national legislation was needed.

---

76. Victoria F. Nourse, In Reckless Hands: Skinner v. Oklahoma and the Near-Triumph of American Eugenics (2008).

77. William Branigin, "Va. Apologizes to the Victims of Sterilizations," Washington Post, May 3, 2002, at B1.

In 1916, the House Labor Committee concluded that "the entire problem has become an interstate problem rather than a problem of isolated States and is a problem which must be faced and solved only by a power stronger than any State."[78] The bill became law on September 1, 1916. Relying on the national power to regulate commerce, it prohibited products of child labor from being shipped interstate. No producer, manufacturer, or dealer could ship or deliver for shipment in interstate or foreign commerce any article produced by children within specified age ranges: under the age of sixteen for products from a mine or quarry, or under the age of fourteen from any mill, cannery, workshop, factory, or manufacturing establishment.[79]

Two years later, a 5–4 Court in *Hammer* v. *Dagenhart* struck down the statute as unconstitutional. The Court ruled that the steps of "production" and "manufacture" of goods were local in origin and therefore not part of "commerce" among the states subject to regulation by Congress.[80] The Court reasoned that although child labor might be harmful, the goods shipped from their efforts "are of themselves harmless."[81] To the majority, the statute encroached on state authority. Efforts to deal with child labor would have to be undertaken by individual states. The dissenters argued that Congress, not the Court, was the agency of government constitutionally authorized to determine and settle these policy questions. They disagreed it was permissible to allow

---

78. H. Rept. No. 46, 64th Cong., 1st Sess. 7 (1916).

79. 39 Stat. 675, sec. 1 (1916).

80. Hammer v. Dagenhart, 247 U.S. 251 (1918).

81. Id. at 272.

regulation "against strong drink but not as against the product of ruined lives."[82]

Members of Congress did not accept this decision as the final word. They prepared legislation to regulate child labor through the taxing power. A federal excise tax would be levied on the net profit of persons employing child labor within prohibited ages.[83] Senator Robert L. Owen introduced a bill identical to the one the Court had invalidated, adding this blunt condition: "Any executive or judicial officer who in his official capacity denies the constitutionality of this act shall ipso facto vacate his office."[84] He denied that the Court possessed a supreme or exclusive role in constitutional interpretation (see Box 3.3).

Box 3.3

Denying Judicial Supremacy

It is said by some that the judges are much more learned and wiser than Congress in construing the Constitution. I can not concede this whimsical notion. They are not more learned; they are not wiser; they are not more patriotic; and what is the fatal weakness if they make their mistakes there is no adequate means of correcting their judicial errors, while if Congress should err the people have an immediate redress; they can change the House of Representatives almost immediately and can change two-thirds of the Senate within four years, while the [federal] judges are appointed for life and are removable only by impeachment.

Source: 56 Cong. Rec. 7433 (1918).

---

82. Id. at 280.
83. 56 Cong. Rec. 8341, 11560 (1918).
84. Id. at 7432.

The child-labor bill based on the taxing power passed Congress and became law in 1919.[85] When the issue reached the Supreme Court, Solicitor General James M. Beck urged the justices to exercise institutional and political prudence when reviewing legislation supported by the elected branches. He said the Philadelphia Convention "voted down any proposition that the judiciary should have an absolute revisionary power over the legislature, which as the representative of the people was regarded as the most direct organ of their will."[86] He further explained that only when a case presents an "*invincible, irreconcilable, and indubitable repugnancy*" between a congressional statute and the Constitution should the Court nullify the statute.[87] He reminded the justices of the consequences of *Dred Scott,* "possibly the principal cause, next to slavery itself, in precipitating the greatest civil war in history."[88] The belief that the Court is empowered to freely override the policy decisions of the elected branches "is a mischievous one, in that it so lowers the sense of constitutional morality among the people that neither in the legislative branch of the Government nor among the people is there as strong a purpose as formerly to maintain their constitutional form of Government."[89] The idea that the Court "is the sole

---

85. 40 Stat. 1138 (1919).

86. "Brief on Behalf of Appellants and Plaintiff in Error," Bailey v. George and Bailey v. Drexel Furniture Co., Supreme Court of the United States, October Term, 1921, Nos. 590, 657, February 1922, reprinted at 21 Landmark Briefs and Arguments of the Supreme Court of the United States: Constitutional Law 45 (Philip B. Kurland & Gerhardt Casper, eds.) (using number at top of page).

87. Id. at 46 (emphases in original).

88. Id. at 48.

89. Id. at 54.

guardian and protector of our constitutional form of government has inevitably led to an impairment, both with the people and with their representatives, of what may be called the constitutional conscience."[90] Through those words, Beck warned that an arrogant Court pretending that it alone has the capacity to interpret the Constitution necessarily leads the public to become alienated from its own national charter.

The Court took no heed of Beck's counsel, striking down the new child-labor law by a majority of 8 to 1. Justice John Hessin Clarke dissented without giving any reason.[91] Congress passed a constitutional amendment in 1924 to give it the power to regulate child labor. By 1937, only twenty-eight of the necessary thirty-six states had ratified it.[92] Beginning in 1937, conservative justices began to retire, giving President Franklin D. Roosevelt his first opportunity to name justices to the Court. With this change in the Court's composition under way, in 1938 Congress passed legislation to regulate child labor, relying on the same power that the Court had invalidated earlier: the commerce power.

In 1941, a thoroughly reconstituted (and chastened) Court not only upheld the new statute, but did so unanimously. Moreover, it proceeded to publicly apologize for the Court's earlier effort to distinguish between the "production" and "manufacture" of goods (regarded as local in origin) and interstate commerce subject to regulation by Congress. Writing for the Court, Chief Justice Harlan Fiske Stone noted:

---

90. Id.

91. Child Labor Tax Case (Bailey v. Drexel Furniture Co.), 259 U.S. 20 (1922).

92. John R. Vile, Encyclopedia of Constitutional Amendments, Proposed Amendments, and Amending Issues, 1789–2002, at 61–63 (2003).

"While manufacture is not of itself interstate commerce, the shipment of manufactured goods interstate is such commerce and the prohibition of such shipment by Congress is indubitably a regulation of the commerce."[93] Congress, he said, "following its own conception of public policy," may exclude from interstate commerce whatever goods it considers injurious to the public health, morals, or welfare, "even though the state has not sought to regulate their use."[94] Constitutional judgments here are to be made by the elected branches, not the judiciary.

Chief Justice Stone deferred fully to the constitutional judgments of members of Congress: "The motive and purpose of a regulation of interstate commerce are matters for the legislative judgment upon the exercise of which the Constitution places no restrictions and over which the courts are given no control." Whatever the legislative motive and purpose, regulations of commerce "which do not infringe some constitutional prohibition are within the plenary power conferred on Congress by the Commerce Clause." He concluded that the congressional prohibition of the shipment of interstate goods produced by child labor "is within the constitutional authority of Congress."[95] Continuing, Stone said that the reasoning offered by the "bare majority" of the Court in *Hammer* v. *Dagenhart* in 1918 "was novel when made and unsupported by any provision of the Constitution."[96] Zero constitutional support—a remarkable indictment of judicial incapacity to interpret the Constitution. Five years

---

93. United States v. Darby, 312 U.S. 100, 113 (1941).

94. Id. at 114.

95. Id. at 115.

96. Id.

after Stone's opinion, the Court admitted that "the history of judicial limitation on congressional power over commerce, when exercised affirmatively, had been more largely one of retreat than of ultimate victory."[97]

13. Sole-Organ Doctrine. In dicta by Justice Sutherland in *United States* v. *Curtiss-Wright Export Corp.* (1936), the Court departed from the core issue presented to it—whether Congress could delegate its power to the president in the field of international relations—and decided to endorse a broad definition of independent, plenary, and inherent presidential power in foreign affairs.[98] Congress passed legislation in 1934 to authorize the president to prohibit the sale of arms in the Chaco region in South America whenever he found that "it may contribute to the reestablishment of peace" between belligerents.[99] At issue was *legislative* power, not executive power. When President Roosevelt issued a proclamation to impose the embargo, he relied solely on the statutory authority given him.[100] He made no claim of inherent or extra-constitutional power.

Litigation on the proclamation focused on legislative power because during the previous year the Court twice struck down a delegation by Congress of domestic power to the president.[101] The issue in *Curtiss-Wright* was therefore whether Congress could delegate legislative power more

---

97. Prudential Ins. Co. v. Benjamin, 328 U.S. 408, 415 (1946).

98. 299 U.S. 304, 319–20 (1936).

99. 48 Stat. 811, ch. 365 (1934).

100. Id. at 1745.

101. Panama Refining Co. v. Ryan, 293 U.S. 388 (1935); Schechter Corp. v. United States, 295 U.S. 495 (1935).

broadly in international affairs than it could in domestic affairs. A district court, holding that the joint resolution impermissibly delegated legislative authority, said nothing about any reservoir of inherent presidential power.[102]

The district court's decision was taken directly to the Supreme Court. None of the briefs on either side discussed the availability of independent, inherent, or plenary powers of the president. The source of power was legislative. Given President Roosevelt's stated dependence on statutory authority and the lack of anything in the briefs about independent executive authority, there was no need for the Court to speak of any power other than that delegated by Congress.

Writing for the Court, Justice Sutherland reversed the district court and upheld the delegation of legislative power. Whether the joint resolution "had related solely to internal affairs" would be open to the challenge of unlawful delegation he found "unnecessary to determine," because the "whole aim of the resolution is to affect a situation entirely external to the United States, and falling within the category of foreign affairs."[103] Certainly the Constitution gives extensive powers over foreign affairs to Congress. Sutherland had to concede that by upholding the joint resolution. That should have been the end of the decision.

Instead, Sutherland decided to tuck into the decision material he had written as a U.S. senator from Utah, an article called "The Internal and External Powers of National Government"[104] In that article, he argued that after the Declaration

---

102. United States v. Curtiss-Wright Export Corp., 14 F.Supp. 230 (S.D.N.Y. 1936).

103. United States v. Curtiss-Wright Export Corp., 299 U.S. at 315.

104. S. Doc. No. 417, 61st Cong., 2d Sess. (1910).

of Independence the power of "national sovereignty" passed from England to the United States, and he associated national sovereignty with the president.[105] But in 1776 there was no president, and one would not take office until 1789. Contrary to Sutherland's argument that the individual states could not exercise the power of national sovereignty,[106] they actually did: making treaties, borrowing money, soliciting arms, laying embargoes, collecting tariff duties, and conducting separate military campaigns.[107] The Supreme Court has recognized that the American colonies, upon their separation from England, exercised the powers of sovereign and independent governments.[108]

In addition to misconceptions and historical errors in his Senate document, Sutherland published a book in 1919 that attempted to distinguish between external and internal affairs.[109] In various places the book concluded that the president "must be given a free, as well as a strong hand" in carrying out military operations, and that it was unacceptable to "rely on the slow and deliberate processes of legislation," for such reliance might "court danger—perhaps overwhelming

---

105. Id. at 3.

106. Id. at 12.

107. Charles Lofgren, "United States v. Curtiss-Wright Export Corporation: An Historical Assessment," 83 Yale L. J. 1 (1973); David M. Levitan, "The Foreign Relations Power: An Analysis of Mr. Justice Sutherland's Theory," 55 Yale L. J. 467 (1946); Claude H. Van Tyne, "Sovereignty in the American Revolution: An Historical Study, "12 Am. Hist. Rev. 529 (1907).

108. E.g., United States v. California, 332 U.S. 19, 31 (1947) and Texas v. White, 74 U.S. 700, 725 (1869).

109. George Sutherland, Constitutional Power and World Affairs 26 (1919).

disaster."[110] None of that had anything to do with the issues in *Curtiss-Wright*. Congress had acted when it passed legislation to deal with the situation in the Chaco; Roosevelt did not act unilaterally. In addition to the articles already cited, other scholars have taken Sutherland to task for twisting historical and constitutional precedents.[111]

Particularly damaging is Sutherland's complete distortion of John Marshall's speech in 1800, when Marshall served as a member of the House of Representatives. Through misconception and misrepresentation, Sutherland created for the president a source of power in foreign affairs that was not grounded in authority delegated by Congress: "It is important to bear in mind that we are here dealing not alone with an authority vested in the President by an assertion of legislative power, but with such an authority plus the very delicate, plenary and exclusive power of the President as the sole organ of the federal government in the field of international relations—a power which does not require as a basis for its exercise an act of Congress, but which,

---

110. Id. at 111.

111. E.g., Roy E. Brownell II, "The Coexistence of United States v. Curtiss-Wright and Youngstown Sheet & Tube v. Sawyer in National Security Jurisprudence," 16 J. Law & Policy 1 (2000); Michael D. Ramsey, "The Myth of Extraconstitutional Foreign Affairs Power," 42 Wm. & Mary L. Rev. 379 (2000); and Michael J. Glennon, "Two Views of Presidential Foreign Affairs Power: Little v. Barreme or Curtiss-Wright?," 13 Yale J. Int'l L. 5 (1988).

These critiques are summarized in Louis Fisher, "Presidential Inherent Power: The 'Sole Organ' Doctrine," 37 Pres. Stud. Q. 139, 149–51 (2007). For a lengthier study: Louis Fisher, "The 'Sole Organ' Doctrine," the Law Library of Congress, August 2006; http://loufisher.org/docs/pip/441.pdf. Accessed Feb. 19, 2013.

of course, like every other governmental power, must be exercised in subordination to the applicable provisions of the Constitution."[112]

In his speech in 1800, Marshall made this remark: "The President is the sole organ of the nation in its external relations, and its sole representative with foreign nations."[113] However, anyone reading the entire speech will understand that Marshall was not advocating inherent, exclusive, plenary, or extra-constitutional powers for the president. His only objective was to defend the actions of President John Adams in carrying out an extradition provision in the Jay Treaty. Adams, of course, was not the sole organ in formulating the treaty. He was, instead, the sole organ in *implementing* it. Article II of the Constitution directs the president to "take Care that the Laws be faithfully executed." Article VI states that all treaties made "shall be the supreme Law of the Land." Following those constitutional provisions, President Adams turned over to the British an individual (Thomas Nash) charged with murder on a British ship.[114]

Later, in his capacity as chief justice, Marshall consistently held that the making of foreign policy is a joint exercise by the legislative and executive branches (through treaties and statutes), not a unilateral and exclusive power of the president. With the war power, for example, he looked solely to Congress—not the president—for constitutional authority to take the country to war. Writing in 1801 for the Court, he

112. 299 U.S. at 319–20.

113. 10 Annals of Cong. 613 (1800), cited by Justice Sutherland (299 U.S. at 319).

114. For background on Marshall's speech in 1800: Fisher's articles in note 111.

explained, "The whole powers of war being, by the constitution of the United States, vested in congress, the acts of that body can alone be resorted to as our guides in this enquiry."[115] In an 1804 case, he ruled that when a presidential proclamation issued in time of war conflicts with a statute enacted by Congress, the statute controls.[116]

The Court acted irresponsibly by permitting Justice Sutherland to add pages of dicta wholly unrelated to the issue presented to it. His colleagues allowed him to include not only dicta, but lengthy passages that were false and highly misleading. Every time the Supreme Court and lower courts cite the sole-organ doctrine from *Curtiss-Wright* favorably and fail to understand what Marshall actually meant, they compound the error and perpetuate an inflated concept of presidential power. Justices and judges (and their law clerks) rarely take the time to read Marshall's speech, and announce that Sutherland clearly misrepresented it. Repeatedly citing Sutherland's dicta without looking at the original source injures the reputation of the judiciary and promotes unchecked, extra-constitutional presidential power.

14. Flag-Salute Case of 1940. By a commanding majority of 8 to 1, in 1940 the Supreme Court upheld a compulsory flag salute in Pennsylvania that forced children to violate their religious beliefs. So defective and unpersuasive was the opinion and so swift the public condemnation that three years later the Court reversed itself. Both cases are discussed in Chapter Five.

---

115. Talbot v. Seeman, 5 U.S. 1, 28 (1801).
116. Little v. Barreme, 2 Cr. (6 U.S.) 170, 179 (1804).

15. Nazi Saboteur Case. In June 1942, eight German saboteurs arrived on the east coast of the United States, placed on shore at night by two submarines. They had been trained to use explosives, fuses, and detonators against railroads, factories, bridges, and other strategic targets in the United States. Within a matter of weeks they were arrested, in large part because two of them—George John Dasch and Ernest Peter Burger—decided to turn themselves in and help the FBI find their colleagues. The initial plan was to prosecute all eight in civil court, but instead they were brought before a military tribunal.

The Supreme Court, in *Ex parte Quirin,* upheld the tribunal's jurisdiction.[117] That decision was cited to justify the military tribunals created by President George W. Bush after September 11, 2001, to try terrorists responsible for the attacks on the World Trade Center and the Pentagon. In a dissent in 2004, Justices Antonin Scalia and John Paul Stevens referred to *Quirin* as "not this Court's finest hour."[118] The defects in the Court's decision in 1942 are quite pronounced. President Bush's claim that he could unilaterally create military commissions, using *Quirin* as a reliable precedent, was rejected by the Court in 2006.[119] What were the fundamental deficiencies of *Quirin*?

Why weren't the eight saboteurs tried in civil court, as planned? Dasch agreed to plead guilty with the understanding that everything would be kept quiet. A day later, when he looked through the slit in his cell door and saw an FBI agent reading a newspaper with Dasch's photo on the front

---

117. 317 U.S. 1 (1942).

118. Hamdi v. Rumsfeld, 542 U.S. 507, 569 (2004).

119. Hamdan v. Rumsfeld, 548 U.S. 557 (2006).

page, he believed he had been betrayed.[120] He now wanted to go into civil court and fully explain his actions in helping the FBI.[121] The administration could not allow that. It had given the American public the impression that superior FBI investigative skills uncovered the plot. President Roosevelt and FBI Director J. Edgar Hoover did not want the public to know how easily German U-boats reached American shores undetected. Civil courts were now ruled out.

There was a second reason for a military tribunal. The statute on sabotage carried a maximum thirty-year penalty, but the government had little confidence it could prevail on that count. The men had not actually committed an act of sabotage. The maximum penalty the Justice Department could point to was three years in prison for an attempt at sabotage.[122] A military tribunal offered many advantages: it could act in secret, move swiftly, and mete out the ultimate penalty: death. President Roosevelt considered the death penalty "almost obligatory."[123]

On July 2, 1942, less than a week after the eight Germans had been apprehended, Roosevelt issued Proclamation 2561 to create a military tribunal.[124] Also on July 2, he issued a military order appointing the members of the tribunal, the prosecutors, and the defense counsel.[125] All seven members

---

120. Transcript of the trial of the Nazi saboteurs, from July 8 to August 1, 1942, National Archives, College Park, Md., at 2546.

121. Id. 677.

122. Francis Biddle, In Brief Authority 328 (1962).

123. Memo from Roosevelt to Biddle, June 30, 1942, PSF, "Departmental File, Justice, 1940–44," Box 56, Franklin D. Roosevelt Library, Hyde Park, N.Y.

124. 7 Fed. Reg. 5101 (1942).

125. Id. at 5003.

of the tribunal were generals, subordinate to Roosevelt. Also subordinate to Roosevelt were the two prosecutors, Attorney General Francis Biddle and Major General Myron C. Cramer, as well as the two defense counsel, Colonels Cassius M. Dowell and Kenneth Royall. After the tribunal completed its work and reached a judgment, the trial record would be transmitted to Roosevelt "for [his] action thereon." The July 2 order vested "final reviewing authority" in Roosevelt. The process was a closed circle, lacking any independent checks.

The military tribunal began without any rules. The tribunal created them when it responded to motions made by the government and defense counsel as the trial progressed.[126] Early in the trial, Royall made clear his intention to take the case to civil court or designate someone from the private sector to do so.[127] After Royall met with Justices Hugo Black and Owen Roberts to discuss the case, Chief Justice Harlan Fiske Stone reached out to other justices and decided the Court would hear oral argument on Wednesday, July 29.[128]

There were several legal problems. No action had been taken by any lower federal court and no one could possibly regard this case as one of original jurisdiction. Royall managed to get the issue to a federal district court in the District of Columbia. On July 28, at 8 p.m., district judge James W. Morris issued a brief statement turning down his request for a *habeas* petition.[129] Oral argument before the Supreme Court began the next day at noon. The justices and their law clerks

---

126. Louis Fisher, Nazi Saboteurs on Trial: A Military Tribunal and American Law 52–53, 54–55, 57–58 (2003).

127. Id. at 20–21.

128. Id. at 67–68.

129. Ex parte Quirin, 47 F.Supp. 431 (D.D.C. 1942).

were not prepared to analyze complex issues of military law and Articles of War that are rarely placed before the Court. The briefs are dated the same day oral argument began. To compensate for the lack of preparation, the Court allowed nine hours for oral argument.

Because there had been no action by the appellate court, the D.C. Circuit, some justices wondered how the Supreme Court could hear the case. After some discussion, Royall agreed to get the papers to the appellate court.[130] On July 31, after two days of oral argument, the Court received the case from the D.C. Circuit. At 11:59 a.m. it officially took the case, and one minute later issued a one-page *per curiam* decision that upheld the jurisdiction of the military tribunal.[131] The decision provided no legal reasoning or justification. The legal community and the public knew what the Court did, but not why it did it. The Court promised to release a full opinion at a later date.[132] The full opinion was not available until nearly three months later: October 29.

The burden of writing the full opinion fell to Chief Justice Stone. His labors increased when the military tribunal completed its work and recommended the death sentence for all eight Germans. The administration decided to give prison sentences to Dasch and Burger and execute the others. Electrocutions were carried out on August 8, just a few days after the *per curiam* decision. Stone realized that nothing in the full opinion could cast doubt on the *per curiam* opinion. Also, he did not want the Court's reputation damaged with

130. Fisher, *supra* note 126, at 96–97.

131. Myron C. Cramer, "Military Commissions: Trial of the Eight Saboteurs," 17 Wash. L. Rev. & St. B. J. 247, 253 (1942).

132. Ex parte Quirin, 317 U.S. 1, 11 (1942).

concurrences and dissents. On September 10, Stone wrote to Justice Felix Frankfurter that it was "very difficult to support the Government's construction of the [Articles of War]." He said it "seems almost brutal to announce this ground of decision for the first time after six of the petitioners have been executed and it is too late for them to raise the question if in fact the articles as they construe them have been violated."[133] Only after the war, Stone observed, would the facts be known, with the release of the tribunal trial transcript and other documents to the public. By that time, Dasch and Burger could raise some questions successfully, which "would not place the present Court in a very happy light."[134]

Stone and the other justices struggled to determine whether President Roosevelt had violated Articles of War 46 and 50½. When the full opinion was released on October 29, it concluded that the secrecy surrounding the trial made it impossible for the Court to judge whether Roosevelt's proclamation and military order violated the Articles of War.[135] Having issued a hasty *per curiam* opinion, the justices were in no position to look too closely at whether Roosevelt had acted inconsistently with the Articles of War. In the words of legal scholar Alpheus Thomas Mason: "Their own involvement in the trial through their decision in the July hearing practically compelled them to cover up or excuse the President's departures from customary practice."[136]

Years later, Justice William Douglas said it was "unfortunate the court took the case." While it was "easy to agree

133. Fisher, *supra* note 126, at 110.

134. Id. at 111.

135. Id. at 113

136. Alpheus Thomas Mason, "Inter Arma Silent Leges: Chief Justice Stone's Views," 69 Harv. L. Rev. 806, 826 (1956).

on the original per curiam, we almost fell apart when it came to write out the views."[137] Justice Frankfurter was sufficiently troubled by the decision to ask Frederick Bernays Wiener, an expert on military law, to offer his views on *Quirin*. Among other points, Wiener spoke about the administration's disregard for "almost every precedent in the books" when it established the tribunal.[138] As for Article of War 46, which required the trial record of a general court-martial or military commission to be referred for review to the staff judge advocate or the judge advocate general, Wiener concluded that Roosevelt ignored that requirement.[139]

These letters from Wiener must have had an impact on Frankfurter. In 1953, when the justices were deciding whether to sit in summer session to hear the espionage case of Ethel and Julius Rosenberg, someone recalled that the Court had sat in summer session in 1942 to hear the Nazi saboteur case. Could the Court once again issue a short *per curiam* opinion and file a full opinion at a later date? Justice Jackson opposed this suggestion, as did Frankfurter, who added that the *Quirin* "experience was not a happy precedent."[140] The procedures followed by the Court in the Nazi saboteur case would not be repeated.

16 & 17. Japanese American Cases. Of the two Japanese American cases decided in 1943 and 1944, only the second decision, *Korematsu,* is singled out by constitutional scholar

---

137. William O. Douglas, The Court Years, 1939–1975, at 138–39 (1981).

138. Fisher, *supra* note 126, at 129.

139. Id. at 130–31.

140. Id. at 134.

Jamal Greene as worthy of being "anticanonical."[141] Yet the case decided the previous year, *Hirabayashi* v. *United States,* is based on the same purely racial grounds for punishing Japanese Americans, two-thirds of whom were U.S. citizens.[142] *Hirabayashi* involved a curfew placed on Japanese Americans on the west coast of the United States. *Korematsu* concerned their placement in detention centers.

Greene notes that *Korematsu* was "based on little more than naked racism and associated hokum," and that the position of General John DeWitt—a major advocate of the curfew and detention policies—proposed that the Japanese be "wiped off the map." Remarkably, DeWitt advised the Secretary of War on February 14, 1942: "The very fact that no sabotage has taken place to date is a disturbing and confirming indication that such action will be taken."[143] With no evidence of disloyalty or subversive activity, and without the benefit of procedural safeguards, the United States imprisoned Japanese Americans solely on grounds of race.

In a dissent in *Korematsu,* Justice Murphy protested that the exclusion order resulted from an "erroneous assumption of racial guilt" found in DeWitt's report, which referred to all individuals of Japanese dissent as "subversives" belonging to "an enemy race" whose "racial strains are undiluted."[144] Murphy dissented from "this legalization of racism."[145] In another dissent, Justice Jackson remarked that "here is an attempt to make an otherwise innocent act a crime merely because this

---

141. Greene, *supra* note 29, at 422–23.

142. Hirabayashi v. United States, 320 U.S. 81 (1943); Korematsu v. United States, 323 U.S. 214 (1944).

143. Id.

144. Korematsu v. United States, 323 U.S. at 235–36.

145. Id. at 242.

prisoner is the son of parents to which he had no choice, and belongs to a race from which there is no way to resign."[146]

Writing for the Court, Justice Black acquiesced to military experts: "We are unable to conclude that it was beyond the war power of the Congress and the Executive to exclude those of Japanese ancestry from the West Coast war area at the time they did."[147] Weigh those words: "We are unable to conclude." Frequently, that phrase is used by a court ready to bow to actions in the field of national security without any plausible and persuasive grounds. Although Jackson dissented, he shared Black's deferential attitude toward executive military judgments (see Box 3.4).

Box 3.4

Deferring to the Military

The limitation under which courts always will labor in examining the necessity of a military order are illustrated by this case. How does the Court know that these orders have a reasonable basis in necessity? No evidence whatever on that subject has been taken by this or any other court. There is sharp controversy as to the credibility of the DeWitt report. So the Court, having no real evidence before it, has no choice but to accept General DeWitt's own unsworn, self-serving statement, untested by any cross-examination, that what he did was reasonable. And thus it will always be when courts try to look into the reasonableness of a military order.

In the very nature of things, military decisions are not susceptible of intelligent judicial appraisal. . . .

Source: Korematsu v. United States, 323 U.S. 214, 245 (1944) (Jackson, J., dissenting).

---

146. Id. at 243.

147. Id. at 217–18.

"Thus it will always be"? It was not always that way before 1944 and certainly was not always that way after 1944. Jackson had an opportunity, as a member of an independent branch, to probe the basis for the exclusion order. He claimed the Court had "no choice." Justices always have a choice. Certainly they had a choice when Jackson described DeWitt's statement as unsworn, self-serving, and untested by cross-examination. The justices had a duty under their oath of office to make this kind of rebuttal: "We decide cases based on evidence. You have provided none, other than crude assertions of racism. Both for the rights of Japanese Americans and our own institutional self-respect, we must hold against the exclusion order." In his dissent, Justice Murphy identified an effective and principled way to challenge executive assertions: "Justification for the exclusion is sought, instead, mainly upon questionable racial and sociological grounds not ordinarily within the realm of expert military judgment."[148] The Court was not faced with what might be called a "military judgment." There was no reason to defer to DeWitt's purely prejudiced and ignorant beliefs about race and sociology.[149]

Three decades after these constitutional violations, the elected branches reevaluated the Japanese American cases. On February 20, 1976, President Gerald Ford issued a proclamation publicly apologizing for the treatment of Japanese Americans, resolving that "this kind of action shall never again be repeated."[150] Congress created a commission to

---

148. Id. at 236–37.

149. Eugene W. Rostow, "The Japanese American cases—A Disaster," 54 Yale L. J. 489 (1945); Nanette Dembitz, "Racial Discrimination and the Military Judgment; The Supreme Court's Korematsu and Endo Decisions," 45 Colum. L. Rev. 175 (1945).

150. Proclamation 4417, 42 Fed. Reg. 7741 (1976).

gather facts to determine the wrongs done by Roosevelt's order. The commission's report, released in December 1982, stated that the order "was not justified by military necessity" and the policies of curfew and detention "were not driven by analysis of military conditions." The factors shaping those decisions were "race prejudice, war hysteria and a failure of political leadership." As a result, "grave injustice" was done to U.S. citizens and resident aliens of Japanese ancestry.[151]

Congress passed legislation in 1988 to establish a trust fund of $1.25 billion to pay up to $20,000 to eligible individuals.[152] No financial payment could possibly compensate for the lost years, humiliation, and economic sacrifices of having to sell property at reduced values when forced to relocate to detention camps. In signing the bill, President Reagan said the larger purpose had less to do with property than with honor: "For here we admit a wrong; here we reaffirm our commitment as a nation to equal justice under the law."[153]

The deficiencies of the two Japanese American cases would be underscored when Gordon Hirabayashi and Fred Korematsu returned to court after newly discovered documents revealed that executive officials had deceived the judiciary. They learned that the executive branch had withheld vital evidence from the courts. At the time of Korematsu's case in 1944, Justice Department attorneys were aware that a 618-page document called *Final Report,* prepared by the War Department for General DeWitt, contained erroneous claims about alleged espionage efforts by Japanese Americans. The FBI and the FCC rejected War Department assertions that

151. Commission on Wartime Relocation and Internment of Civilians. Personal Justice Denied 18 (1982).

152. 102 Stat. 903, 905–06, secs. 104–05 (1988).

153. Public Papers of the Presidents, 1988, II, at 1054.

some Japanese Americans had sent signals from shore to assist Japanese submarine attacks along the Pacific coast.

Justice Department officials had a professional obligation to inform the judiciary about those false allegations. A footnote in the Justice Department brief for *Korematsu* should have clearly identified the errors and misconceptions that appeared in the *Final Report*. Instead, the footnote was so watered down that the courts could not possibly have understood the extent to which the administration had misled them.[154] A district court in 1984 concluded that the executive branch had "knowingly withheld information from the courts when they were considering the critical question of military necessity in this case."[155] To the court, there was "substantial support in the record that the government deliberately omitted relevant information and provided misleading information in papers before the court."[156] On that basis, the district court vacated Korematsu's conviction. The Justice Department did not appeal that decision.

Hirabayashi also challenged his conviction for violating the curfew order. The Justice Department had argued that the government lacked time to separate loyal Japanese Americans from those who might be subversive. It did not claim it was impossible to distinguish between loyal and disloyal Japanese. However, General DeWitt believed that because of racial ties, filial piety, and strong bonds of common tradition, culture, and customs, it was "impossible to establish the identity of

---

154. Peter Irons, Justice at War: The Story of the Japanese American Internment Cases 278 (1983).

155. Korematsu v. United States, 584 F.Supp. 1406, 1417 (D. Cal. 1984).

156. Id. at 1420.

the loyal and the disloyal with any degree of safety."[157] For DeWitt, there was no "such a thing as a loyal Japanese."[158] The draft report contained his remarks. The final report, after War Department editing, did not. The Justice Department received the final report but not the draft version.

In 1986, a district court ruled that although the Justice Department "did not knowingly conceal" from Hirabayashi's counsel and the Supreme Court the racial grounds DeWitt offered for excluding Japanese, it was necessary to charge the executive branch with concealment because the information had been known to the War Department, an arm of government. The failure of the executive branch to disclose DeWitt's position "was an error of the most fundamental character." Hirabayashi "was in fact seriously prejudiced by that non-disclosure in his appeal from his conviction for failing to report."[159] The district court vacated that conviction but declined to vacate the one for violating the curfew order.[160] On appeal, the Ninth Circuit vacated both convictions.[161] The Supreme Court has never overruled its decisions in *Hirabayashi* and *Korematsu*.[162]

The capacity of the executive branch to deceive the judiciary would be replayed in the state secrets litigation

---

157. Hirabayashi v. United States, 627 F.Supp. 1445, 1449 (W.D. Wash. 1986).

158. Id. at 1452.

159. Id. at 1457.

160. Id. at 1457–58.

161. Hirabayashi v. United States, 828 F.2d 591 (9th Cir. 1987).

162. However, see the "Confession of Error" by Acting Solicitor General Neal Katyal, posted on May 20, 2011. He summarizes the mistakes made by the Solicitor General in the Japanese American cases. http://blogs.justice.gov/main/archives/1346. Accessed Feb. 19, 2013.

that reached the Supreme Court in *United States* v. *Reynolds* (1953), discussed at the start of the next chapter. The George W. Bush and Obama administrations invoked the doctrine of state secrets repeatedly after the terrorist attacks of September 11 to diminish judicial independence in reviewing executive branch actions. The courts could have insisted on an independent role to check constitutional violations, but once again they deferred to executive claims and failed to allow private plaintiffs to pursue their cases. After analyzing *Reynolds,* the next chapter moves to rulings on school busing, *Roe* v. *Wade,* a federalism decision that became unworkable, legislative vetoes, sodomy statutes, the presidential election of 2000, and two campaign finance cases (*Buckley* v. *Valeo* and *Citizens United*).

CHAPTER FOUR

JUDICIAL FAILINGS AFTER WORLD WAR II

The previous chapter covered several judicial "wounds" incurred through World War II. This chapter analyzes other Supreme Court failings from 1945 to 2012. The issues: the state secrets doctrine, school busing, abortion, federalism, legislative vetoes, sodomy statutes, the presidential election of 2000, and campaign expenditures. Reasons for these selections include executive deceptions of the judiciary (state secrets), widespread public opposition (school busing), untenable framework (*Roe* v. *Wade*), unworkable federalism theory (*National League of Cities* v. *Usery*), failure to understand executive-legislative accommodations (the legislative veto case), trying to settle disputes over sexual behavior (sodomy statues), selecting a president (*Bush* v. *Gore*), and using legal fictions in campaign expenditure cases (*Buckley* and *Citizens United*). Court cases on individual and minority rights from the 1870s to the 1960s are examined in Chapter Five.

18. State Secrets. After the terrorist attacks of September 11, 2001, the Bush administration relied on the "state secrets privilege" to deny private litigants access to executive branch documents that might have revealed constitutional violations by the CIA and other agencies. When Barack Obama entered the White House, his administration also argued that these lawsuits would endanger national security if litigants and federal judges were permitted to examine certain executive documents. The executive branch relies heavily on *United States v. Reynolds* (1953), the first time the Supreme Court recognized the state secrets privilege in its full scope. On October 6, 1948, a B-29 lost control at 20,000 feet over Waycross, Georgia, and exploded. Killed in the blast were five of eight crewmen and four of five civilian engineers who served as technical advisers on confidential equipment. Three widows of the civilian engineers, acting under the Federal Tort Claims Act of 1946, sued the government for negligent and wrongful acts.[1] In a tort claims case, courts have a duty to examine evidence from both sides.[2]

In district court in Pennsylvania, attorneys for the three widows submitted a number of interrogatories to the government. They asked whether the government had prescribed modifications for the B-29 to prevent overheating of the engines to reduce fire hazards, and requested details of any modifications that had been carried out. To those questions the government answered "No."[3] When the three families discovered the declassified accident report in 2000 they realized the government's answer was false.[4]

District Judge William Kirkpatrick decided on June 30, 1950, that the accident report on the B-29 crash was not

---

1. 60 Stat. 843, sec. 403(1) (1946).

2. Id., at § 410(a).

3. Transcript of Record, Supreme Court of the United States, October Term, 1952, No. 21, United States v. Reynolds, at 14.

4. For access to the accident report: www.fas.org/sgp/othergov /reynoldspetapp.pdf. Accessed Feb. 19, 2013.

"privileged."[5] The Secretary of the Air Force, Thomas K. Finletter, issued a statement about state secrets and the accident report without saying explicitly that state secrets were in the report. Kirkpatrick directed the government to give him the accident report to be read in his chambers. When the government refused, he ruled for the widows. On December 11, 1951, a unanimous Third Circuit upheld his decision. If it allowed the privilege, it said, it would be a small step "to assert a privilege against the disclosure of records merely because they might prove embarrassing to government officers."[6] To permit the government as a party to "conclusively determine the Government's claim of privilege is to abdicate the judicial function and permit the executive branch of the Government to infringe the independent province of the judiciary as laid down by the Constitution."[7] The judiciary had protected its independent role, but not for long.

The Supreme Court Decides.   In its brief to the Supreme Court, the executive branch continued to muddle the basic issue: Did the accident report contain state secrets? The government wrote: "To the extent that the report reveals military secrets concerning the structure or performance of the plane that crashed or deals with these factors in relation to projected or suggested secret improvements it falls within the judicially recognized 'state secret' privilege."[8] "To the extent"? Did the report contain state secrets or not? That question could be

---

5. Brauner v. United States, 10 F.R.D. 468, 472 (D. Pa. 1950).

6. Reynolds v. United States, 192 F.2d 987, 995 (3d Cir. 1951).

7. Id. at 997.

8. Brief for the United States, United States v. Reynolds, No. 21, U.S. Supreme Court, October Term, 1952, at 45.

answered only if the Court read the report, which it chose not to do.

For a 6–3 Court, Chief Justice Fred Vinson announced incoherent principles of judicial responsibility: "The court itself must determine whether the circumstances are appropriate for the claim of privilege, and yet do so without forcing a disclosure of the very thing the privilege is designed to protect."[9] Disclosure to the public is a legitimate concern, but there is no such risk if justices read the accident report in their chambers. By deciding not to examine the report, the Court could not possibly determine "whether the circumstances are appropriate for the claim of privilege." The Court accepted at face value a self-serving statement by the executive branch, an assertion that turned out to be false. Vinson offered two extreme positions, implying he was seeking something in the middle (see Box 4.1).

Box 4.1

Vinson's Two Broad Propositions

We have had broad propositions pressed upon us for decision. On behalf of the Government it has been urged that the executive department heads have power to withhold any documents in their custody from judicial review if they deem it to be in the public interest. Respondents have asserted that the executive's power to withhold documents was waived by the Tort Claims Act. Both positions have constitutional overtones which we find it unnecessary to pass upon, there being a narrower ground for decision....

Source: United States v. Reynolds, 345 U.S. 1, 6 (1953).

---

9. United States v. Reynolds, 345 U.S. at 8.

By failing to look at the accident report and accepting the government's claim that it contained state secrets, Vinson essentially accepted the first broad proposition. He argued that Secretary Finletter attempted "to invoke the privilege against revealing military secrets, a privilege which is well established in the law of evidence."[10] That was not Finletter's objective. The report contained no military secrets. Vinson drew attention to a fundamental constitutional principle: "Judicial control over the evidence in a case cannot be abdicated to the caprice of executive officers."[11] Abdication occurs whenever a judge fails to look at evidence. He then said, inconsistently: "Yet we will not go so far as to say that the court may automatically require a complete disclosure to the judge before the claim of privilege will be accepted in any case."[12] Abdication occurs whenever a judge fails to look at evidence.

Through his disjointed reasoning, Vinson deliberately placed courts in an inferior institutional position. Without looking at the accident report, the Court could not independently evaluate the merits of a privilege claimed by an executive official. Nor could it protect the rights of the three widows. The Court surrendered to the executive branch fundamental judicial duties in deciding questions of privilege and access to evidence. By refusing to examine the report, the Court took the risk of being hoodwinked by the executive branch. As it turned out, it was. Four decades later, the government declassified the accident report. It contains no state secrets. It does reveal government negligence. The

---

10. Id. at 6–7.

11. Id. at 9–10.

12. Id. at 10.

executive branch misled the Court in 1953 just as it did in the Japanese American cases.

In its brief in the 1953 *Reynolds* case, the Justice Department attempted to add legitimacy to the state secrets privilege by citing two early precedents: the Aaron Burr trial of 1807 and a Civil War case that involved a spy for President Lincoln.[13] The Burr case adds no support for the state secrets privilege. The Civil War case is wholly unrelated to the lawsuit brought by the three widows.

The Burr Trial. On December 6, 1806, President Jefferson informed Congress about the plans of several private citizens to carry out a military expedition against territories of Spain.[14] He said it would be inappropriate and unjust to name particular individuals involved in the conspiracy, given the mix of rumors and conjecture, but did not hesitate to identify "the principal actor, whose guilt is placed beyond question."[15] He regarded Aaron Burr as "the prime mover" and referred to three letters from General James Wilkinson as evidence.

Burr, accused of a criminal offense that carried the death penalty, had every right to subpoena the Wilkinson letters to determine their credibility and worth. According to the government's brief in the *Reynolds* case, "Jefferson ignored the subpoena" and the court "avoided the ultimate test of power with the executive."[16] The brief further claimed that whenever disclosure of information to plaintiffs "would be detrimental

---

13. Brief for the United States, United States v. Reynolds, No. 21, Supreme Court of the United States, at 32–33, 36, 42 (September 1952).

14. 1 Richardson 394.

15. Id. at 400.

16. Brief for the United States, United States v. Reynolds, at 32.

to the public interest . . . the determination of the executive is conclusive."[17] All three statements are false. The government may not charge and convict someone of a criminal offense on the basis of secret evidence. The government has a choice: give a defendant the evidence or do not prosecute.

Chief Justice John Marshall, presiding over the trial as part of his circuit duties, said he would deplore any action by him to deny an accused the information needed to rebut the government's charges.[18] He gave the government a choice: give Burr the letters or drop the charges. Jefferson directed government prosecutors to provide the letters to Burr.[19] On September 1, 1807, the jury found Burr not guilty on the charge of treason.[20] The court then considered seven counts of a misdemeanor charge. Again Burr and his attorneys were able to examine various documents.[21] The jury returned with a judgment of "not guilty."[22] Contrary to the government's brief in *Reynolds,* the decision about access to documents in a criminal case was not made "conclusively" by the executive. Those determinations were made by Chief Justice Marshall.

---

17. Id. at 33.

18. United States v. Burr, 25 Fed. Cas. 30, 37 (C.C.D. Va. 1807) (No. 14,692d).

19. United States v. Burr, 25 Fed. Cas. 55, 65, 68–69, 74–75, 85 (C.C.D. Va. 1807) (No. 14,693); 9 The Writings of Thomas Jefferson 61n (Ford, ed., 1898).

20. United States v. Burr, 25 Fed. Cas. at 180–81 (C.C.D. Va. 1807) (No. 14,693).

21. Id. at 189, 190–92.

22. Id. at 201. For further details on the Burr case: Louis Fisher, In the Name of National Security: Unchecked Presidential Power and the Reynolds Case 212–20 (2006).

Lincoln's Spy. The government's brief in *Reynolds* also cited the case of *Totten v. United States* (1875).[23] The Supreme Court, in 1953, described the government's attempt to invoke the state secrets privilege as one "well established in the law of evidence."[24] Among the cases cited by the Court (and listed first): *Totten.* It has some relevance to the state secrets privilege, but only to a very narrow set of cases. It had no relevance to the case brought by the three widows.

President Lincoln entered into a private contract with William A. Lloyd, directing him to travel behind Confederate lines to collect military information. Lloyd was to be paid $200 a month, but received funds only to cover his expenses. After he died, his family sued to recover compensation for his services. The Supreme Court rejected the lawsuit on the basis that many areas of private life remain confidential, including persons who contract for secret services with the government, saying the "existence of a contract of that kind is itself a fact not to be disclosed."[25] *Totten* had no application to the *Reynolds* case. The *Totten* principle covers lawsuits involving private individuals who enter into secret contracts with the government. In this type of case, courts regularly dismiss claims by litigants seeking funds or assistance they thought they were entitled to.[26]

Fraud against the Court. In 2000, the three widows obtained a copy of the declassified accident report.[27] When their

---

23. Brief for the United States, note 16, at 36n, 42.

24. United States v. Reynolds, 345 U.S. 1, 6–7 (1953).

25. Totten v. United States, 92 U.S. 105, 107 (1875).

26. E.g., Tucker v. United States, 118 F.Supp. 371 (Ct. Cl. 1954); Simrick v. United States, 224 Ct. Cl. 724 (1980); Mackowski v. United

attorneys read the report, they realized it contained no state secrets. Moreover, it revealed that the government had been negligent by not installing heat shields in the B-29 to avoid overheating of the engines. The Air Force committed other negligent acts.[28] The families decided to file a new lawsuit: not for tort claims this time, but for a writ of *coram nobis,* charging that the executive branch had misled the judiciary and committed fraud against it.[29] They filed the writ with the Supreme Court, but the Court declined to take it. They had to start over in district court.[30]

One might expect federal courts to strongly oppose any effort by the executive branch (which appears in court more than any other party) to deceive the judiciary and weaken its independent role. However, when the three families returned to court to charge fraud against the judiciary, they were entirely unsuccessful. The widows lost in district court on September 10, 2004, and their appeal to the Third Circuit failed on September 22, 2005.[31] On May 1, 2006, the

---

States, 228 Ct. Cl. 717 (1981), cert. denied, 454 U.S. 1123 (1981); Tucker v. United States, 118 F. Supp. 371 (Ct. Cl. 1954); Guong v. United States, 860 F.2d 1063 (Fed. Cir. 1988); Kielzynski v. U.S. C.I.A. 128 F.Supp.2d 141 (E.D. N.Y. (2001); Monarch Assur. P.L.C. v. United States, 42 Fed. Cl. 258, 264 (1998); Monarch Assur. P.L.C. v. United States, 36 Fed. Cl. 324 (1996); Monarch Assur. P.L.C. v. United States, 244 F.3d. 1356 (Fed. Cir. 2001); Tenet v. Doe, 544 U.S. 1 (2005). For details on those cases: Fisher, *supra* note 22, at 223–27.

27. Fisher, *supra* note 22, at 166–67.

28. Id. at 178–79.

29. For examples of *coram nobis* lawsuits, see id. at 169–76.

30. Id. at 176–88.

31. Herring v. United States, 424 F.3d 384 (3d Cir. 2005). Details of these two decisions are provided in Fisher, *supra* note 22, at 274–77.

Supreme Court denied cert.[32] The constitutional value given short shrift in this writ of *coram nobis* is the need to protect the integrity, independence, and reputation of the federal judiciary. When the Supreme Court accepted the government's claim in 1953 without examining the accident report, it functioned as an arm of the executive branch. When courts operate in that manner, litigants and citizens lose faith in the judiciary, the rule of law, the adversary system, and the constitutional principle of checks and balances.

Long-Term Impact of Reynolds. The flawed analysis of *Reynolds* continues to damage the judiciary after September 11, 2001, in both the Bush and Obama administrations. After the 9/11 attacks, the Bush administration invoked the state secrets privilege to block efforts by private citizens to gain access to agency documents about constitutional violations in several areas, including warrantless surveillance and the policy of "extraordinary rendition" used to transfer individuals to other countries for interrogation and torture.[33] When Barack Obama became president, his administration used the same state secrets privilege against private lawsuits. Both administrations advised federal courts that private suits could not proceed without jeopardizing national security and foreign policy.

A typically listless, apathetic ruling was issued by the Ninth Circuit on September 8, 2010, in *Mohamed* v. *Jeppesen Dataplan, Inc.* Plaintiffs wanted information on the "torture flights" conducted by the CIA with the assistance of a private contractor. A decision by the Ninth Circuit *en banc* reflects

---

32. Herring v. United States, 547 U.S. 1123 (2006).

33. Louis Fisher, The Constitution and 9/11: Recurring Threats to America's Freedoms 248–84, 321–60 (2008).

the incoherent ruling issued by the Supreme Court in *Reynolds*. The Ninth Circuit said it "must make an independent determination whether the information is privileged," claiming that federal courts "take very seriously our obligation to review the [government's claims] with a very careful, indeed a skeptical eye."[34] Sounds good. Those promises of judicial independence were then discarded with this statement: "We acknowledge the need to defer to the Executive on matters of foreign policy and national security and surely cannot legitimately find ourselves second guessing the Executive in this arena."[35] Under that reading, the executive branch may commit illegal and unconstitutional acts without an independent judicial check and without an opportunity for private plaintiffs to pursue their cases.

19. School Busing. The Supreme Court's desegregation decision in *Brown* v. *Board of Education* (1954) did little to integrate public schools. Part of the delay came from the loose guidelines issued by the Court the next year, in a second *Brown* v. *Board of Education* (1955), directing states to move "with all deliberate speed."[36] As late as 1964, the Court complained: "There has been entirely too much deliberation and not enough speed" in enforcing *Brown*.[37] Two years later, a federal appellate court remarked: "A national effort, bringing together Congress, the executive and the judiciary may be able to make meaningful the right

---

34. Mohamed v. Jeppesen Dataplan, Inc., 614 F.3d 1070, 1080 (9th Cir. 2010), citing Al-Haramain Islamic Found., Inc. v. Bush, 507 F.3d 1190, 1202 (9th Cir. 2007); 614 F.3d at 1082.

35. 614 F.3d at 1081–82.

36. 349 U.S. 294, 301 (1955).

37. Griffin v. School Bd., 377 U.S. 218, 229 (1964).

of Negro children to equal educational opportunities. *The courts acting alone have failed.*"[38]

For much of the 1950s and 1960s, some Northerners believed that school segregation was a problem only in the South. Yet many Northern school systems were segregated not by law, but by fact. Increasingly, inner-city blacks were encircled by white suburbs. What might be done when segregated schools result from residential patterns and family income? To the courts, busing offered one option. In 1971, a unanimous Court held that district courts possessed broad power to fashion remedies to desegregate schools. To achieve greater racial balance, judges could alter school district lines, reassign teachers, and bus students.[39]

That same year a unanimous Court struck down state antibusing laws.[40] Those rulings clashed with language in the Civil Rights Act of 1964, which defined desegregation as the assignment of students to public schools without regard to their race, color, religion, or national origin. However, desegregation "shall not mean the assignment of students to public schools in order to overcome racial imbalance."[41] The statute did not empower a federal official or court "to issue any order seeking to achieve a racial balance in any school by requiring the transportation of pupils."[42]

Busing spread to non-Southern states. A Supreme Court decision in 1973 covered the school system in Denver,

---

38. United States v. Jefferson County Board of Education, 372 F.2d 836, 847 (5th Cir. 1966) (emphasis in original).

39. Swann v. Charlotte-Mecklenburg Bd. of Ed., 402 U.S. 1 (1971).

40. North Carolina State Board of Education v. Swann, 402 U.S. 43 (1971).

41. 78 Stat. 246, sec. 401(b) (1964).

42. Id., sec. 407(a).

Colorado. Parents of black children charged that the school board maintained a segregated system by using student attendance zones, school site selection, and a neighborhood school policy. A 7–1 Court concluded that the school board intended school segregation, resulting in *de jure* segregation. Several justices dismissed the difference between *de jure* and *de facto* segregation. To them, the existence of segregated public schools provided *prima facie* evidence of a constitutional violation by the school board. They hoped to avoid having to decide whether segregated schools resulted from "intent" (*de jure*) or "effect" (*de facto*).[43]

Court-ordered busing affected Detroit.[44] Lower courts decided that the problem could not be solved by focusing only on the city. Widespread busing, reaching to suburban areas, was required. Previous Court decisions, either unanimous or with a 7–1 majority, now gave way to split decisions. A 5–4 Court in 1974 dismissed the remedies proposed by lower courts and decided that a cross-district busing plan would disrupt school district lines, interfere impermissibly with local school control, and put judges in the role of "school superintendent," for which they lacked qualification. A district court had ordered the school board to obtain at least 295 school buses, to be financed by the state. Further, the Court objected that a metropolitan-area solution punished outlying districts without any evidence they had committed constitutional violations.[45] Three years later, a unanimous Court supported lower courts that had ordered compensatory

43. Keyes v. School District No. 1, Denver, Colo., 413 U.S. 189 (1973).

44. Joyce A. Baugh, The Detroit School Busing Case: Milliken v. Bradley and the Controversy over Desegregation (2011).

45. Milliken v. Bradley, 418 U.S. 717 (1974).

or remedial educational programs for children subject to past acts of *de jure* segregation. Special help did not rely on busing, but rather on extra instruction for reading, training for teachers, testing, and counseling.[46]

Two other Northern school systems, in Columbus and Dayton, Ohio, came under Supreme Court scrutiny. Because there had been *de jure* segregation, school officials had to take affirmative steps to desegregate. Chief Justice Warren Burger remarked: "It is becoming increasingly doubtful that massive public transportation really accomplishes the desirable objectives sought."[47] Justice Lewis Powell, in a dissent, warned that parents resentful of court-ordered integration might withdraw their children from public schools by relocating ("white flight"), or enroll them in private schools. Either action would lead to resegregation of public schools.[48] Powell observed that people "instinctively resent coercion," particularly when it affects their children and their educational opportunities.[49] Justice William Rehnquist dissented, with Potter Stewart joining in part.

To constitutional scholar Jeffrey Rosen, court-ordered busing "produced a firestorm of resistance from the president and Congress that never abated."[50] A Gallup poll in 1973 found a clear majority of Americans backing integration but only 5 percent supporting busing.[51] Court-ordered

---

46. Milliken v. Bradley, 433 U.S. 267 (1977).

47. Columbus Board of Education v. Penick, 443 U.S. 449, 469 (1979).

48. Id. at 484.

49. Id. at 489. See also Dayton Board of Education v. Brinkman. 433 U.S. 406 (1977), and Dayton Board of Education v. Brinkman, 443 U.S. 526 (1979).

50. Jeffrey Rosen, The Most Democratic Branch: How the Courts Serve America 67 (2006).

51. Id. at 68.

busing reflected "judicial unilateralism of the most aggressive kind."[52] Confronted by congressional and presidential opposition, federal judges "proved unable and ultimately unwilling to impose an unpopular and destabilizing social reform on their own."[53]

In 1982, the Court split 5–4 in reviewing a statewide initiative in Washington designed to prohibit the use of mandatory busing to achieve integrated schools. The Court found the initiative in violation of the Equal Protection Clause.[54] A combination of an increasingly divided Court, public opposition, and congressional restrictions eventually forced the judiciary to abandon widespread busing as a remedy for desegregation. Neither black parents nor white parents wanted their children transported long distances to achieve a court-ordered plan to desegregate schools. They preferred other solutions, including "magnet schools" that offered extra teachers, computers, better laboratories, and other resources. With the support of the Supreme Court, some communities abandoned busing as an instrument for racially integrating their schools.[55]

20. Roe v. Wade. Public officials and private citizens are often asked if they support the Supreme Court's abortion

---

52. Id. at 69.

53. Id.

54. Washington v. Seattle School Dist. No. 1, 458 U.S. 457 (1982).

55. Riddick v. School Bd. of City of Norfolk, 784 F.2d 521 (4th Cir. 1986) (*en banc*), cert. denied, 479 U.S. 938 (1986). See also Parents Involved in Community Schools v. Seattle School District No.1, 551 U.S. 701 (2007). For close analysis of the political difficulties of school busing: J. Harvie Wilkinson III, From Brown to Bakke: The Supreme Court and School Integration: 1954–1978, at 131–239 (1979).

opinion in *Roe* v. *Wade* (1973). The question is not helpful unless it asks two separate issues: (1) "Do you support a woman's right to choose?" and (2) "Do you support the Court's trimester framework that assigns different rights to women during their first, second, and third trimesters of pregnancy?" There is broad support for the former and very little for the latter. Both liberals and conservatives criticized the Court for issuing an opinion more appropriate for a legislative body or executive agency. Years later, in *Planned Parenthood* v. *Casey* (1992), the Court acknowledged its mistake in trying to legislate in such detail and jettisoned the trimester framework.

The question before the Court in *Roe* was complex and politically charged. How could abortions be performed within a legal structure that satisfied the competing values of those who wanted abortion on demand and those who believed equally strongly in an embryo's right to life? Various states wrestled with the issue. It became a national controversy when the Court decided to "settle it" for the entire country. The decision represented a serious political and institutional miscalculation. As legal analyst Linda Greenhouse has noted, the manner in which the Court handled the issue deeply split the nation and gave "rise to the religious Right,"[56] a political intervention that continues to this day.

Justice Harry Blackmun wrote for a 7–2 Court, with Justices Byron White and William Rehnquist in dissent. Concurrences were written by Justices Potter Stewart and William O. Douglas and by Chief Justice Burger. The Court struck down a Texas statute that prohibited abortion except on medical advice for the purpose of saving the mother's life. It held that a woman's right to privacy, whether found in

---

56. Linda Greenhouse, The U.S. Supreme Court: A Very Short Introduction 78 (2012).

the Fourteenth Amendment or the Ninth Amendment, "is broad enough to encompass a woman's decision whether or not to terminate her pregnancy."[57] It disagreed that a woman "is entitled to terminate her pregnancy at whatever time, in whatever way, and for whatever reason she alone chooses."[58] It accepted as "reasonable and appropriate" for a state to decide that at some point in time it may legislate to protect the health of the mother and potential human life.[59]

In *Roe,* the Court attempted to draw precise boundaries: "The common law found greater significance in quickening," a stage when the fetus is beginning to move and the woman is about to deliver.[60] Whatever existed in common law centuries ago did not reflect medical knowledge in 1973, as the Court would gradually discover. Justice Blackmun defined the stage at which a fetus may survive (viability) "as usually placed at about seven months (28 weeks) but may occur earlier, even at 24 weeks."[61] To Blackmun, the interests of the mother vary over the course of pregnancy. He noted that the "compelling" point for the woman, in "the light of present medical knowledge, is at approximately the end of the first trimester."[62]

Blackmun decided the state's compelling interest was "at viability," which he took to mean the ability of a fetus to survive "outside the mother's womb."[63] However, medical technology was rapidly changing the concept of viability, with the fetus able to survive outside the mother's womb at much

---

57. Roe v. Wade, 410 U.S. 113, 153 (1973).
58. Id.
59. Id. at 159.
60. Id. at 160.
61. Id.
62. Id. at 163.
63. Id.

earlier stages. Blackmun wrote that abortion in the first trimester, "although not without its risk, is now relatively safe."[64] Any state interest in protecting a woman from the hazards of an abortion, "except when it would be equally dangerous for her to forgo it, has largely disappeared."[65] Thereafter, the state "retains a definite interest in protecting the woman's own health and safety when an abortion is proposed at a late stage of pregnancy."[66]

In a dissent, Rehnquist objected that "the conscious weighing of competing factors that the Court's opinion apparently substitutes for the established test is far more appropriate to a legislative judgment than to a judicial one."[67] Similarly, the Court's decision "to break pregnancy into three distinct terms and to outline the permissible restrictions the State may impose in each one … partakes more of judicial legislation than it does of a determination of the intent of the drafters of the Fourteenth Amendment."[68] White, in a dissent printed in the companion case of *Doe* v. *Bolton,* remarked: "As an exercise of raw judicial power, the Court perhaps has authority to do what it does today; but in my view its judgment is an improvident and extravagant exercise of the power of judicial review that the Constitution extends to this Court."[69]

An early critique of *Roe* v. *Wade* by legal scholar John Hart Ely identified some of its principal weaknesses. Blackmun's opinion consisted of "drawing lines with an apparent precision one generally associates with a commissioner's regulations.

---

64. Id. at 149.

65. Id.

66. Id. at 150.

67. Id. at 173.

68. Id. at 174.

69. 410 U.S. 179, 222 (1973).

On closer examination, however, the precision proves largely illusory."[70] Ely said if he were a legislator he would vote for a statute "very much like the one the Court ends up drafting."[71] His praise is somewhat overstated. Elsewhere he noted that the concept of viability "will become even less clear than it is now as the technology of birth continues to develop."[72] To Ely, "the problem with *Roe* is not so much that it bungles the question it sets itself, but rather that it sets itself a question the Constitution has not made the Court's business."[73]

Support for the trimester framework continued to erode, in part because Sandra Day O'Connor joined the Court in 1981. In a lengthy dissent two years later, she objected that the trimester or "three-stage" approach was "completely unworkable."[74] As a result of advances in medical technology, she noted that the majority now recognized that "the safety of second-trimester abortions has increased dramatically."[75] The *Roe* framework "is clearly on a collision course with itself."[76] In 1986, Rehnquist replaced Burger as chief justice and Antonin Scalia took Rehnquist's seat as associate justice, adding another opponent of *Roe* and one far more critical than O'Connor. After Anthony Kennedy replaced Justice Powell in 1988, the Court was in a position to overhaul and possibly overrule *Roe*.

---

70. John Hart Ely, "The Wages of Crying Wolf: A Comment on Roe v. Wade," 82 Yale L. J. 920, 922 (1973).

71. Id. at 926.

72. Id. at 924.

73. Id. at 943.

74. Akron v. Akron Center for Reproductive Health, 462 U.S. 416, 454 (O'Connor, J., dissenting).

75. Id. at 454, citing 435–56.

76. Id. at 458.

The changed composition of the Court was evident in a 1989 decision. It reviewed a Missouri statute that imposed a number of restrictions on a woman's decision to have an abortion. Without overruling *Roe,* a plurality opinion by Rehnquist, White, and Kennedy rejected the trimester framework.[77] Scalia would have repealed all of *Roe.*[78] O'Connor saw no need in this case to reexamine the constitutional validity of *Roe,* but said she continued to consider the trimester framework as "problematic."[79] In 1992, the Court finally abandoned the framework. An opinion by O'Connor, Kennedy, and David Souter specifically rejected it.[80] Stevens and Blackmun disagreed with the rejection. In their separate opinion, Rehnquist, White, Scalia, and Clarence Thomas stated that *Roe* "was wrongly decided," apparently agreeing with the framework's rejection without expressly saying so.[81] Scalia, in a separate opinion, discussed the deficiencies of the entire *Roe* decision.[82]

What was learned from *Roe* v. *Wade*? Writing in 1985 while serving on the D.C. Circuit, Ruth Bader Ginsburg said the decision became "a storm center" and "sparked public opposition and academic criticism," in part "because the Court ventured too far in the change it ordered and presented an incomplete justification for its action."[83] Instead of simply

---

77. Webster v. Reproductive Health Services, 492 U.S. 490, 517–20 (1989).

78. Id. at 537.

79. Id. at 525, 529.

80. Planned Parenthood of Southeastern Pa. v. Casey, 505 U.S. 833, 869–79 (1992).

81. Id. at 944.

82. Id. at 982–1002.

83. Ruth Bader Ginsburg, "Some Thoughts on Autonomy and Equality in Relation to Roe v. Wade," 63 N.C. L. Rev. 375, 376 (1985).

striking down the Texas law, "the most extreme prohibition extant," the decision (along with the companion case of *Doe* v. *Bolton*) "called into question the criminal abortion statutes of every state, even those with the least restrictive provisions."[84] The "sweep and detail of the opinion stimulated the mobilization of a right-to-life movement and an attendant reaction in Congress and state legislatures."[85] In 1992, after the Court rejected the trimester framework and she was confirmed as associate justice, Ginsburg offered additional views about *Roe* (see Box 4.2).

Box 4.2

Ginsburg Reflects on *Roe* v. *Wade*

Judges play an interdependent part in our democracy. They do not alone shape legal doctrine, but ... they participate in a dialogue with other organs of government, and with the people as well.... Measured motions seem to me right, in the main, for constitutional as well as common law adjudication. Doctrinal limbs too swiftly shaped, experience teaches, may prove unworkable. The most prominent example in recent decades is *Roe* v. *Wade*....

The seven to two judgment in *Roe* v. *Wade* declared "violative of the Due Process Clause of the Fourteenth Amendment" a Texas criminal abortion statute that intolerably shackled a woman's autonomy; the Texas law "except[ed] from criminality only a *life-saving* procedure on behalf of the [pregnant woman]." Suppose the Court had stopped there ... and had not gone on, as the Court did in *Roe*, to fashion a regime blanketing the subject, a set of rules that displaced virtually every state law then in force.... A less encompassing *Roe* ... might have served to reduce rather than to fuel controversy.

Source: Ruth Bader Ginsburg, "Speaking in a Judicial Voice," 67 N.Y.U. L. Rev. 1185, 1198–99 (1992) (emphasis in original).

---

84. Id. at 380, 381.
85. Id. at 381.

21. Federalism. In *National League of Cities* v. *Usery* (1976), the Supreme Court decided that Congress could not adopt federal minimum-wage and maximum-hour provisions that displaced state powers.[86] The Court's theory of federalism could not be consistently understood and applied in either the lower courts or by the Court itself. After nine years of confusion and frustration, Justice Blackmun switched sides and pronounced the Court's doctrine unworkable.

The Fair Labor Standards Act of 1938 expressly exempted all states and their political divisions from federal minimum-wage and overtime provisions. In 1966, however, Congress extended federal minimum wages and overtime-pay standards to state-operated hospitals and schools. Two years later, in *Maryland* v. *Wirtz*, the Court upheld the statute as rationally based, concluding that Congress had properly taken into account the effect on interstate competition and the promotion of labor peace.[87] Building on that policy, the Court in 1975 upheld the short-term power of the president to stabilize the wages and salaries of state employees.[88]

This mutual accord between the Court and the elected branches came to an abrupt halt in 1976. Justice Rehnquist was able to attract four justices to his position that federal policy had invaded state powers. The Court now decided that the independent status of the states needed to be preserved for "traditional government functions" such as fire prevention, police protection, sanitation, public health, and parks and recreation.[89] *National League of Cities* overruled *Wirtz* by

---

86. 426 U.S. 833.
87. Maryland v. Wirtz, 392 U.S. 183 (1968).
88. Fry v. United States, 421 U.S. 542, 549–59 (1975).
89. National League of Cities v. Usery, 426 U.S. 833 (1976).

holding that a congressional statute in 1974, extending wage-and-hour provisions to almost all state employees, threatened the independent existence of states. It marked the first time in four decades that the Court invalidated a statute passed by Congress pursuant to the Commerce Clause.

Justices William J. Brennan, Jr., White, Marshall, and Stevens wrote sharply worded dissents. In a tentative concurrence, Blackmun supplied the fifth vote to give Rehnquist a majority. Blackmun said he was "not untroubled" by some aspects of the Court's position, but agreed to offer his support.[90] Over the next few years, with evidence mounting that Rehnquist's theory of federalism could not be defended, Blackmun would prepare an opinion overturning *National League of Cities.*

The major problem lay with Rehnquist's assumption that a line could be clearly drawn between traditional and nontraditional government functions. The Supreme Court decided it would not, or could not, draw that line. It delegated that task to the lower courts. A district court did not feel capable of determining the difference between the two functions. Instead, it asked the Labor Department to identify nontraditional state functions. It did so, supplying a list of traditional functions as well.[91] Included in the list of nontraditional functions was "local mass transit systems," which eventually sparked new litigation to challenge *National League of Cities.*

Year after year, lower courts and the Supreme Court tried to figure out what was traditional and nontraditional. Year after year they failed. In 1981, a unanimous Court rejected

---

90. Id. at 856.

91. Neal Devins and Louis Fisher, The Democratic Constitution 67–68 (2004).

a district court's argument that land-use regulation was a "traditional governmental function" reserved to the states.[92] A year later, the Court reviewed a district court's attempt to use *National League of Cities* to prohibit Congress from regulating retail sales of electricity and natural gas. The district court regarded this area of economic regulation as traditional. The Court said it was not.[93]

And so it went. In 1982, the Court rejected the Second Circuit's decision that a state-owned railroad engaged in interstate commerce carried out a traditional function. A unanimous Court disagreed, pointing out that the operation of railroads "has traditionally been a function of private industry, not state or local governments."[94] A case that reached the Court in 1983 involved a decision by a district court involving Wyoming's mandatory retirement of game wardens at the age of fifty-five. Game wardens, to the district court, seemed to fit the categories of police protection, parks, and recreation, and therefore represented a traditional state function. A 5–4 Court reversed the district court.[95] Significantly, Blackmun provided the fifth vote in this case. There seemed to be little life remaining in the federalism doctrine announced in *National League of Cities*.

By 1985, Blackmun had had enough. His opinion in *Garcia* v. *San Antonio Metropolitan Transit Authority* nullified Rehnquist's opinion issued nine years earlier. Blackmun

---

92. Hodel v. Virginia Surface Mining & Recl. Assn., 452 U.S. 264 (1981).

93. FERC v. Mississippi, 456 U.S. 742 (1982).

94. United Transportation Union v. Long Island R. Co., 455 U.S. 678, 686 (1982).

95. EEOC v. Wyoming, 460 U.S. 226 (1983).

explained the difficulties that courts experienced trying to determine the difference between traditional and nontraditional functions. In one example, a district court decided that municipal ownership and operation of a mass-transit system was a traditional governmental function. Three federal appellate courts and one state appellate court reached the opposite conclusion.[96] The effect of Blackmun's 5–4 decision was to take this element of federalism away from the judiciary and leave it with the political process of Congress. He rejected "as unsound in principle and unworkable in practice, a rule of state immunity from federal regulation that turns on a judicial appraisal of whether a particular governmental function is 'integral' or 'traditional.'"[97] To Blackmun, the Court in *National League of Cities* "tried to repair what did not need repair."[98]

22. Legislative Vetoes. In an effort to control delegated authority, Congress experimented with "legislative vetoes" to disapprove certain actions by the executive branch. They do not become public law because they are not submitted to the president. Disapprovals may be exercised by both houses (a concurrent resolution), by either house (a simple resolution), or by committees and subcommittees. In general, concurrent resolutions merely express the opinion of Congress. They are not legally binding. Article I, Section 7, of the Constitution requires that every resolution or vote of the two houses (except on a question of adjournment) be presented to the president. Fundamental to this legislative process are two

---

96. Garcia v. San Antonio Metro. Transit Auth., 469 U.S. 528, 530 (1985).

97. Id. at 546–47.

98. Id. at 557.

principles: bicameralism (both houses must act) and presentment (for the president to sign or veto). An exception to
that process is the adoption of constitutional amendments.
They go directly to the states for ratification rather than to
the president. That procedure, sanctioned by Article V, was
upheld by the Supreme Court in 1798.[99]

From an early date, however, Congress acted by simple
resolution, concurrent resolution, committee, and subcommittee to control executive actions. Various administrations
found those departures not only acceptable, but advantageous.
Legislative vetoes have a complex history and cannot be
described simply as congressional encroachments on executive power. Presidents and Attorneys General did more than
tolerate them and acquiesce. They often invited and encour-
aged their growth to receive the delegations they wanted.[100]

In *INS* v. *Chadha* (1983), the Supreme Court reviewed
a statute that authorized the Attorney General to suspend
the deportation of aliens of good character. The legislation
allowed either house of Congress to disapprove a suspension.
The Court declared the one-house veto unconstitutional
because it violated the Article I requirements of bicameralism
and presentment. Chief Justice Burger, joined by five justices,
announced that whenever congressional action has the "purpose and effect of altering the legal rights, duties, and relations
of persons" outside the legislative branch, Congress must act
through both houses in a bill submitted to the president.[101]
In this manner, the Court supposedly invalidated all forms

---

99. Hollingsworth v. Virginia, 3 Dall. 378 (1798).

100. Louis Fisher, Defending Congress and the Constitution 189–93
(2011).

101. INS v. Chadha, 462 U.S. 919, 952 (1983).

of legislative veto: one-house, two-house, committee, and subcommittee.

Following the Court's decision, Congress has continued to put committee vetoes in bills and have them enacted. Presidents in their signing statements regularly treat committee vetoes as invalid under *Chadha* and lacking in legal effect. Yet executive agencies continue to meet with designated committees to seek their approval before shifting money to new areas. How can that be? The Court decided a constitutional issue and presidents announce their administrations will comply with *Chadha*. Did Congress and executive agencies decide to act in contempt of the Constitution and the Court's authority to interpret it? A better answer is that the Court in *Chadha* did not know what it was doing and did not understand the various political accommodations that were in place when it decided the case. Agencies seek committee approval because they are directed to do so by their budget manuals. Legislative vetoes flourished because they offered important advantages to both Congress and the executive branch. I predicted in 1982 that a Supreme Court decision that invalidated legislative vetoes would not stop them.[102]

Here are some early examples of elected branch accommodations. In 1854, Attorney General Caleb Cushing reasoned that a simple resolution could not coerce a department head "unless in some particular in which a law, duly enacted, has subjected him to the direct action of each; and in such case it is to be intended, that, by approving the law, the president has consented to the exercise of such coerciveness on the part

---

102. Louis Fisher, "Congress Can't Lose on Its Veto Power," Washington Post, February 21, 1982; www.loufisher.org/docs/lv/legveto82.pdf. Accessed Feb. 19, 2013.

of either House."[103] The executive branch saw the virtues even of committee vetoes. Legislation in 1867 placed the following restriction on an appropriation of $35,000 to pay for completing repairs and furnishing of the White House: "*Provided,* That no further payments shall be made on any accounts for repairs and furnishing the executive mansion until such accounts shall have been submitted to a joint committee of Congress, and approved by such committee."[104]

Why would the executive branch share decision-making authority with a joint committee? Why didn't the president veto the committee veto? The answer: presidents and their advisers appreciated the benefits. If the administration reached the statutory limit of $35,000 and wanted to go beyond it, there was no need to seek additional funds by passing another law through both houses and clearing a conference committee. Obtaining approval from the joint committee would suffice.

Presidential Resistance and Acquiescence. On occasion, legislative vetoes faced opposition from the executive branch. In 1920, President Woodrow Wilson vetoed a bill that allowed the Joint Committee on Printing to prescribe regulations for government publications.[105] In that same year he vetoed a bill that allowed Congress to remove by concurrent resolution the Comptroller General and Assistant Comptroller General. After the House of Representatives failed to override the veto, the bill was changed to require a joint resolution for congressional action.[106] Joint resolutions are submitted to the

103. 6 Op. Att'y Gen. 680, 683 (1854).

104. 14 Stat. 469 (1867).

105. H. Doc. No. 764, 66th Cong., 2d Sess. 2 (1920).

106. 59 Cong. Rec. 8609–14 (1920); 42 Stat. 20, 23–24, sec. 303 (1921).

president; concurrent resolutions are not. In 1933, Attorney General William D. Mitchell regarded as unconstitutional a bill that authorized the Joint Committee on Internal Revenue Taxation to make the final decision on any tax refund in excess of $20,000.[107] Acting on the advice of his Attorney General, President Herbert Hoover vetoed the bill and the House failed to override.[108]

Far from being a steadfast opponent of legislative vetoes, Hoover championed them. Facing the Great Depression in 1929, he wanted to reorganize the executive branch to achieve "economy and efficiency." He doubted that his proposals would survive the many hurdles of the legislative process, including amendments and bills never acted on. Therefore he recommended that Congress authorize him to reorganize the executive branch on this condition: he could act only "upon the approval of a joint committee of Congress."[109] In 1932, Congress enacted legislation with a one-house veto to be exercised within a sixty-day period. If lawmakers failed to block his proposals during that time limit, his proposals would become law even though Congress never acted. In December, the House took a single vote to reject all of his proposals.[110]

President Franklin D. Roosevelt adopted inconsistent positions on the legislative veto, sometimes opposing it and on other occasions accepting it. His administration often waived constitutional objections for practical reasons and the desire for additional statutory authority.[111] Committee vetoes

107. 37 Op. Att'y Gen. 56 (1933).

108. 76 Cong. Rec. 2449 (1933).

109. Public Papers of the Presidents, 1929, at 432.

110. 76 Cong. Rec. 2103–26 (1932).

111. Louis Fisher, "The Legislative Veto: Invalidated, It Survives," 56 Law & Contemp. Prob. 273, 280–82 (1993).

developed in the 1940s in response to emergency conditions
of World War II. It became impractical for Congress to continue the practice of authorizing each defense installation
and public-works project. As a substitute, the administration
submitted certain proposals in advance to be approved by the
Naval Affairs Committee in each house.[112] With that legislative safeguard in place, Congress passed general authorization
statutes in lump sums without specifying individual projects.
By 1944, Congress had written that understanding into law.[113]
Additional "coming into agreement" provisions were added
in 1949 and 1951, requiring the executive branch to obtain
the approval of the Armed Services Committees for the
acquisition of land and real estate transactions.[114] Presidents
at times resisted these committee vetoes, only to acquiesce
in their use.[115]

President Dwight D. Eisenhower learned about the
intricacies of legislative vetoes and their constitutionality. His
Attorney General issued an opinion that the committee veto
represented an unconstitutional infringement of executive
duties.[116] Undeterred, Congress adopted another procedure
that yielded precisely the same legislative control. It drafted
a bill to prohibit appropriations for certain real-estate transactions unless the Public Works Committees first approved
contracts the administration wanted to enter into. Eisenhower signed the bill after being assured that this procedure,
based on the separate legislative stages of authorization and

---

112. 89 Cong. Rec. 1217–29 (1943).

113. 58 Stat. 7–8, 189–90 (1944).

114. 63 Stat. 66 (1949); 65 Stat. 365 (1951).

115. Public Papers of the Presidents, 1951, at 280; 65 Stat. 336, 365,
sec. 601 (1951).

116. 41 Op. Att'y Gen. 230 (1955).

appropriation, was fully within the constitutional authority of Congress to adopt its own rules.[117]

The Chadha Decision. A case that reached the Supreme Court in 1983 involved a procedure that allowed the Attorney General to suspend deportations subject to a two-house veto, later changed to a one-house veto.[118] Prior to this legislation, the only available relief for aliens about to be deported was passage of a private bill, requiring action by both houses. Delays in the legislative process meant deportation. The executive branch was pleased to receive this new authority and uttered no constitutional objections about the legislative veto.

The Court ruled in 1983 that the one-house veto used against Jagdish Chadha was unconstitutional because it violated the requirements of bicameralism and presentment. Chief Justice Burger, joined by five justices, held that whenever congressional action has the effect of altering the legal rights and duties of persons outside the legislative branch, Congress must act through both houses in a bill submitted to the president.[119] That principle was far too broad. As the Justice Department acknowledges, each house of Congress may alter the legal rights and duties of individuals outside the legislative branch without resorting to bicameral action and presentation. The issuance of committee subpoenas is one method.[120] The Court itself had long recognized the power of either house to issue subpoenas and hold uncooperative executive officials

---

117. Joseph P. Harris, Congressional Control of Administration 230–31 (1964).

118. 54 Stat. 670, 671–73, sec. 20 (1940); 66 Stat. 163, 214–17, sec. 244 (1952).

119. INS v. Chadha, 462 U.S. 919, 952 (1983).

120. 20 Op. O.L.C. 124, 138 (1996).

and private citizens in contempt.[121] Impeachment is another way the House of Representatives can affect someone outside the executive branch without bicameralism and presentment.

In *Chadha,* Burger insisted that the framers wanted congressional power exercised "in accord with a single, finely wrought and exhaustively considered, procedure." The records of the Philadelphia convention and ratification debates, he said, provide "unmistakable expression of a determination that legislation by the national Congress be a step-by-step, deliberate and deliberative process."[122] His account was highly abstract and far removed from actual procedures. Both houses of Congress are at liberty to suspend their rules, operate by unanimous consent, place legislative riders on appropriations bills, attach unrelated amendments to bills, and even pass bills that have never been sent to committee.[123]

Burger concluded that the Constitution did not allow Congress "to repeal or amend laws by other than legislative means pursuant to Art. I."[124] By exercising the one-house veto in the deportation case, Congress was not repealing or amending the law. It was following it. The law was effectively amended when the Court deleted the legislative veto but allowed the authority of the Attorney General to remain in force. That was contrary to the intent and expectation of the elected branches when they agreed on the statute. In

---

121. Subpoena power: Eastland v. United States Servicemen's Fund, 421 U.S. 491, 505 (1975); contempt power: Anderson v. Dunn, 6 Wheat. 204 (1821).

122. INS v. Chadha, 462 U.S. at 951, 959.

123. Walter J. Oleszek, Congressional Procedures and the Policy Process (8th ed., 2011).

124. 462 U.S. at 954, n.18.

receiving authority to suspend deportations, the executive branch accepted the one-house veto.

Legislative Vetoes Continue. The Court's theory of government was too much at odds with practices developed over the years by the elected branches. Neither agency officials nor lawmakers accept the static, abstract, and artificial model presented by the Court. Executive officials want substantial latitude in administering delegated authority; lawmakers insist on maintaining control without having to pass another statute. Nothing in *Chadha* displayed any understanding of the political accommodations that had been entered into over the decades, which permitted government to function more effectively with appropriate legislative checks. Whatever the Court decided in *Chadha* would not interrupt understandings entered into by the elected branches.

The majority in *Chadha* did not realize that denying Congress the legislative veto would not automatically empower the president. Instead of a one-house veto over executive reorganization proposals, Congress could insist on a joint resolution of approval. Such a statute fully satisfies bicameralism and presentment, but the burden on the president radically shifts. Instead of one house having to take the initiative to disapprove a reorganization plan, the president needs to gain the approval of both houses within a specified number of days. If one house decides not to approve, the practical effect is a one-house veto. Congress adopted that model a year after *Chadha,* requiring a joint resolution of approval for reorganization plans.[125] Congress could adopt a joint resolution of approval for other areas of delegated

---

125. 98 Stat. 3192 (1984).

authority, including arms sales, national emergencies, and specific agency regulations.

Presidents continue to object to committee vetoes in bills presented to them. In their signing statements, they consider the procedures contrary to *Chadha* and instruct agencies to ignore requirements for committee prior approval.[126] However, agency budget manuals explicitly require committee approval for certain movement of funds. Agency officials honor those manuals because to do otherwise would poison crucial relationships with authorizing and appropriation committees and provoke statutory retaliations and budget cutbacks.[127] The Supreme Court had no understanding that long-standing procedures foster more workable government.[128]

23. Sodomy Statutes. States have attempted to criminalize homosexuality by passing laws that prohibit "crimes against nature," "buggery," "deviancy," and sodomy. Sometimes they borrowed from English common law to define the offense as a crime against nature, either with man or beast. Frequently those laws were challenged as vague, unenforceable, and an invasion of privacy. It was often unclear whether the laws applied only to homosexuals or to heterosexuals, including married couples, as well.

---

126. E.g., President Obama's signing statement on December 23, 2011.

127. Louis Fisher, Obama's Objections to Committee Veto Misguided, Roll Call, January 19, 2012; http://loufisher.org/docs/lv/comveto.pdf. Accessed Feb. 19, 2013.

128. For details on agency budget manuals that require agencies to seek committee approvals for certain types of actions, see Louis Fisher, "Committee Controls of Agency Decisions," Congressional Research Service, Report RL33151, November 16, 2005; http://loufisher.org /docs/lv/2626.pdf. Accessed Feb. 19, 2013.

For cases in which the activity involved male homosexuals or a husband and wife, and where there was no issue of force or coercion, legal action was successful in striking down the statute or reversing a conviction.[129] However, a state sodomy statute proscribing "the abominable and detestable crime against nature, either with mankind or beast," was found by a unanimous Supreme Court in 1973 to be not unconstitutionally vague when applied to two adult males.[130] Opponents of sodomy statutes acknowledged that states had legitimate interests if the activity involved minors, unwilling participants, or actions that took place in public.[131] If consenting adults committed sodomy in private and allowed their activity to become known to a minor, the state could convict them on that ground.[132]

In *Bowers* v. *Hardwick* (1986), a 5–4 Supreme Court sustained a Georgia statute that criminalized sodomy. Michael Hardwick was arrested for engaging in sex with another male adult in his apartment. After the district attorney decided not to present the matter to a grand jury, Hardwick challenged the statute as it applied to private, consensual sodomy. Joining as plaintiffs in the action were "John and Mary Doe," who stated their wish to engage in sexual activity proscribed by the statute. The Eleventh Circuit decided they lacked standing but concluded that the statute violated Hardwick's fundamental rights. It relied on a number of Supreme Court opinions, including *Roe* v. *Wade*.[133]

---

129. Buchanan v. Batchelor, 308 F.Supp. 729 (N.D. Tex. 1970); Cotner v. Henry, 394 F.2d 873 (7th Cir. 1968).

130. Wainwright v. Stone, 414 U.S. 21 (1973).

131. "Statement as to Jurisdiction," Buchanan v. Wade, U.S. Supreme Court, October Term, 1959, at 8.

132. Lovisi v. Slayton, 363 F.Supp. 620 (E.D. Va. 1973).

133. Bowers v. Hardwick, 478 U.S. 186, 189 (1986).

The Supreme Court reversed, holding that the Constitution does not confer a fundamental right upon gay adults to engage in sodomy in private. It claimed that the lawsuit did not require a judgment on whether laws against sodomy between consenting adults "are wise or desirable."[134] Nor was there any question about the right of state legislatures to repeal their laws that criminalize homosexual sodomy or of state court decisions that invalidated those laws on state constitutional grounds.[135] The majority, however, was satisfied that proscriptions against sodomy, whether by homosexuals or married couples, "have ancient roots" dating back to English common law.[136]

Why did the Court take the case? It could have left the Eleventh Circuit's opinion in place and at the state level instead of trying to "settle" the matter for the entire country. Why be guided by English common law and American precedents dating from the 1700s? Public and legislative attitudes about sodomy were clearly changing. The Court should have let the issue remain at the state level, subject to varying legislative and judicial interpretations. As with *Roe,* there was no need to announce an overarching and controlling federal position. To the Court, it was "at best, facetious" to claim that a right to engage in sodomy is "deeply rooted" in America's history or "implicit in the concept of ordered liberty."[137] That same argument could have been leveled at a woman's right to choose abortion, particularly in the early months of pregnancy. Nonetheless, the Court found no "rational basis" for homosexuals to engage in sodomy in the

---

134. Id. at 190.
135. Id.
136. Id. at 192.
137. Id. at 194.

privacy of their homes, even though the law "is constantly based on notions of morality."[138] Those notions were being reexamined in America.

A concurrence by Chief Justice Burger remarked that proscriptions against sodomy "have very 'ancient roots.'"[139] The same could be said of prohibiting women to vote, to practice law, and to exercise financial autonomy. Ancient roots justified slavery and laws against interracial marriage. Burger found nothing in the Constitution "depriving a State of the power to enact the statute challenged here."[140] Nothing in the Constitution deprived Georgia of the power to rescind the statute, either. A number of state courts, including those of New York and Pennsylvania, had already invalidated statutes that criminalized consensual sodomy.[141] Other states would do the same: Kentucky in 1992, Tennessee in 1996, Montana in 1997, Georgia in 1998, and Arkansas in 2002.[142]

Justice Powell, in a concurrence, added the key fifth vote. Shortly after the decision, he admitted he switched his vote to form the majority upholding Georgia's statute.[143] He suggested that Hardwick might have been protected by the

---

138. Id. at 196.

139. Id.

140. Id. at 197.

141. People v. Onofre, 415 N.E.2d 936 (N.Y. 1980); Commonwealth v. Bonadio, 415 A.2d 47 (Pa. 1980).

142. Commonwealth v. Wasson, 842 S.W.2d 487 (Ky. 1992); Campbell v. Sundquist, 926 S.W.2d 250 (Tenn. App. 1996); Gryczan v. State, 942 P.2d 112 (Mont. 1997); Powell v. State, 510 S.E.2d 18 (Ga. 1998); and Jegley v. Picado, 80 S.W.3d 332 (Ark. 2002).

143. Al Kamen, "Powell Changed Vote in Sodomy Case," Washington Post, July 13, 1986, at A1; Ruth Marcus, "Powell Sees No Major Shift," Washington Post, August 13, 1986, at A4.

Eighth Amendment had he been tried, convicted, and sentenced, but the state did not prosecute him.[144] The Georgia statute authorized imprisonment for up to twenty years for a single private, consensual act of sodomy, which to Powell created "a serious Eighth Amendment issue."[145] In delivering a lecture at New York University Law School in 1990 after he retired from the Court, Powell admitted about *Bowers*: "I think I probably made a mistake in that one."[146]

A dissent by Blackmun, Brennan, Marshall, and Stevens avoided the Eighth Amendment and the Equal Protection Clause and focused instead on Hardwick's claim that the Georgia statute "interferes with constitutionally protected interests in privacy and freedom of intimate association."[147] They pointed out that it "took but three years for the Court to see the error in its analysis" in the 1940 compulsory flag-salute case, *Minersville School District* v. *Gobitis,* and hoped the Court would soon reconsider its holding in Hardwick's case.[148] Stevens, Brennan, and Marshall wrote a separate dissent.

The overruling arrived seventeen years later in *Lawrence* v. *Texas* (2003), striking down a Texas sodomy statute. Unlike the case from Georgia, Texas charged and convicted two men who had engaged in a sexual act in a private residence. The Court's composition had changed significantly. Two members of the *Bowers* majority (White and Powell) were replaced by Ruth Bader Ginsburg and Anthony Kennedy.

---

144. Bowers v. Hardwick, 478 U.S. at 197–98.

145. Id. at 197.

146. John C. Jeffries, Jr., Justice Lewis F. Powell: A Biography 530 (2001 ed.). For instructive detail on Powell's difficulty in deciding how to vote on *Bowers,* see id. at 511–30.

147. Bowers v. Hardwick, 478 U.S. at 202.

148. Id. at 213–14.

Both voted against the Texas law. O'Connor, part of the *Bowers* majority, concurred in *Lawrence* by finding the Texas statute invalid on equal-protection grounds because it punished homosexuals but not heterosexuals. Rehnquist served as the new chief justice. His position of associate justice was taken by Antonin Scalia. Rehnquist and Scalia dissented in the 2003 ruling, along with Thomas, who had replaced Marshall. Brennan and Blackmun, dissenters in *Bowers*, were succeeded by David Souter and Stephen Breyer, both voting against the Texas statute.

Although the *Lawrence* majority was 6–3 in striking down the Texas law, it was only 5–4 in overruling *Bowers*. A concurrence by O'Connor stated: "I joined *Bowers*, and do not join the Court in overruling it."[149] She agreed the Texas statute banning same-sex sodomy was unconstitutional. Instead of relying on the Fourteenth Amendment's Due Process Clause, as the Court did in *Lawrence*, she based her position on the Fourteenth Amendment's Equal Protection Clause.Because the Texas statute banned homosexual sodomy but not heterosexual sodomy, she found a violation of equal protection.[150] Scalia's dissent, joined by Rehnquist and Thomas, noted that *Lawrence* did not overrule the holding in *Bowers* that homosexual sodomy is not a "fundamental right."[151]

24. Presidential Election of 2000. A decision by the Supreme Court in *Bush* v. *Gore* (2000) in effect gave the presidency to George W. Bush. To understand the propriety of this decision, it is necessary to review the presidential contest

149. Lawrence v. Texas, 539 U.S. 558, 579 (O'Connor, J., concurring).
150. Id. at 582.
151. Id. at 594.

in 1876 between Rutherford B. Hayes (Republican) and Samuel Tilden (Democrat). It produced 165 electoral votes for Hayes and 184 for Tilden, leaving Tilden one vote short of a majority. Each claimed the remaining twenty disputed votes in South Carolina.[152] Both parties engaged in vote fraud. The number of votes cast in South Carolina far exceeded the number of potential voters.[153] South Carolinians voted repeatedly at different polling places. Additionally, there was little doubt that blacks had been "forcibly prevented from getting anywhere near the polls, where the federal supervisors were stationed."[154]

In Congress Democrats controlled the House, and Republicans the Senate. Unable to resolve the dispute, Congress passed legislation on January 29, 1877, to create an Electoral Commission consisting of five members from the House, five from the Senate, and five justices of the Supreme Court. Four justices were designated by name in the statute. It was their duty to pick the fifth justice.[155] Because the House delegation was divided between three Democrats and two Republicans, and the Senate between three Republicans and two Democrats, and with four justices equally divided between Republicans and Democrats, the fifth justice would function as the tiebreaker.[156]

---

152. Ari Hoogenboom, The Presidency of Rutherford B. Hayes 31 (1988).

153. Michael F. Holt, By One Vote: The Disputed Presidential Election of 1876, at 181 (2008).

154. Id. at 186.

155. 19 Stat. 227, 228, ch. 37 (1877).

156. Edward S. Corwin, The President: Office and Powers, 1787–1957, at 43 (4th ed. 1957).

The initial plan was to select Justice David Davis, whose partisan leanings were sufficiently unclear that he might bring a measure of impartiality. Yet he became the Greenback candidate for a seat in the U.S. Senate and was replaced by Justice Joseph P. Bradley, a Republican from New Jersey. Republicans now had an 8–7 majority on the commission. A series of 8–7 votes awarded Hayes electoral votes from Florida, Louisiana, Oregon, and South Carolina, lifting his total to 185, enough to win the presidency. House Democrats mounted a filibuster, but Hayes eventually took office.

The experience of the 1876 election, marred by fraud, voter intimidation, and the partisan result of the Electoral Commission, convinced Congress to adopt a more credible process. Several principles guided lawmakers. First, they understood that at various times the two houses would be controlled by different political parties, producing tie votes between the two chambers. Second, Congress believed that states should count electoral votes, provided they supplied authenticating documents. Third, Congress needed an expeditious process. Normal deliberative methods were too slow and uncertain. Finally, Congress did not want to repeat the experience of 1876 and leave the final choice to justices of the Supreme Court.[157]

The result of this legislative effort was the Electoral Count Act of 1887, which fixed a day for the meeting of Electors of the president and vice president to provide for and regulate the counting of votes. States would submit certificates of their electoral votes to Congress. The president of the Senate could call for objections. Objections had to be made in writing and

157. Stephen A. Siegel, "The Conscientious Congressman's Guide to the Electoral Count Act of 1887," 56 Fla. L. Rev. 542 (2004).

signed by at least one senator and one member of the House. Objections could also be raised in the House. By concurrent action, the two houses of Congress were empowered to reject certain electoral votes. This joint meeting could not adjourn until the count of electoral votes was complete and the results declared.[158]

By enacting this statute, Congress intended that future disputes over electoral votes should not be referred to outside commissions, including those controlled by justices of the Supreme Court. Electoral disputes were to be settled by the legislative branch. The 1887 statute is referred to as a "safe harbor" law. If a state provides a final determination of any controversy or contest concerning the appointment of its Electors, and the determination is made at least six days before the time set for the meeting of Electors, its determination "shall be conclusive."[159] Through those procedures, the selection of the president remained in the hands of elected members of Congress.

Bush v. Gore. The constitutional problems of 1876 resurfaced in the presidential race of 2000. Once again a disputed vote prevented the candidates—George W. Bush and Al Gore—from obtaining a majority of electoral votes. Once again the winner would be effectively decided not by the elected members of Congress, but by justices of the Supreme Court. The manner in which the Court reached its decision provoked strong objections from four dissenting justices and from conservative and liberal scholars.

---

158. 24 Stat. 373 (1887).

159. 3 U.S.C. § 5. For early analysis of this statute, see John W. Burgess, "The Law of the Electoral Count," 3 Pol. Sci. Q. 633 (1888).

Initially, Bush received 246 electoral votes and Gore 267. They needed a majority: 270. The result depended on 25 electoral votes in Florida. From election day (November 7) to December 12, the outcome remained uncertain. Various rulings were handed down by lower courts in Florida, federal district courts, the Eleventh Circuit, the Florida Supreme Court (four times), and the U.S. Supreme Court (twice).[160] The Florida legislature and the U.S. Congress waited to exercise their constitutional duties. On December 12, a 5–4 Court ruled against a recount of Florida votes requested by Gore, and Gore gave a concession speech the following day.[161] On January 6, 2001, a joint session of Congress tallied the electoral votes that made Bush the next president.

The 5–4 ruling began with a brief *per curiam* opinion followed by a concurrence by Rehnquist (joined by Scalia and Thomas). Dissents came from Stevens (joined by Ginsburg and Breyer) and by Souter (joined by Breyer and Stevens, and Ginsburg in part). The fragmentation of the Court left few clues of legal principles that might be applied to future presidential contests. Why did the Court decide the case instead of leaving it to established statutory procedures? Sections 5 and 15 of Title 3, drawn from the Electoral Count Act of 1887, directed the states to take specified steps. If they did, their results would be treated as "conclusive" when Congress met to receive electoral votes. The purpose of the 1887 statute was to place the final decision with elected officials in the legislative, not the judicial, branch.

---

160. Louis Fisher and Katy J. Harriger, American Constitutional Law 970–79 (10th ed. 2013).

161. Bush v. Gore, 531 U.S. 98 (2000).

Academic Evaluations. A vast amount of literature analyzed the Court's decision.[162] Many of the critiques have been properly described as academic ranting. To constitutional scholar David Ryden, "it is difficult to recall another instance in which the scholarly opinions and analysis appeared to derive directly from commentators' respective partisan or ideological dispositions."[163] Political scientist Jeff Polet remarked that for "all the charges of partisanship that have been leveled against the Court, one would be hard-pressed not to conclude that the same can be said of virtually all the commentary."[164]

The conservative and liberal blocs in *Bush* v. *Gore* presented some unusual configurations. As Ryden observed, the majority "exhibited a newfound fondness for the Equal Protection Clause, creatively manipulating it to stop the recounts," while the liberals "were transformed into the new caretakers of federalism and judicial restraint; their new best

---

162. E.g., Charles L. Zelden, Bush v. Gore: Exposing the Hidden Crisis in American Democracy (2008); David K. Ryden, ed., The U.S. Supreme Court and the Electoral Process (2002); E. J. Dionne, Jr. and William Kristol, eds., Bush v. Gore: The Court Cases and the Commentary (2001); Howard Gillman, The Votes That Counted: How the Court Decided the 2000 Presidential Election (2001); Samuel Issacharoff, et al., When Elections Go Bad: The Law of Democracy and the Presidential Election of 2000 (2001); Richard A. Posner, Breaking Deadlock: The 2000 Election, the Constitution, and the Courts (2001); Jack N. Rakove, ed., The Unfinished Election of 2000: Leading Scholars Examine America's Strangest Election (2001); and Cass R. Sunstein and Richard A. Epstein, eds., The Vote: Bush, Gore, and the Supreme Court (2001).

163. David K. Ryden, "Out of the Shadows: Bush v. Gore, The Court, and the Selection of a President," in The U.S. Supreme Court and the Electoral Process 224 (Ryden, ed., 2002).

164. Jeff Polet, "The Imperiousness of Bush v. Gore," in The U.S. Supreme Court and the Electoral Process 263 (Ryden, ed., 2002).

friends were legislatures rather than courts."[165] Critics who rebuked the Court for deciding a "political question" offered no objections to favorable rulings by the Florida Supreme Court for Gore.

Federal judge Richard A. Posner defended the Court's decision in part because he lacked confidence in the capacity of Congress to handle this type of issue. In his judgment, Congress "is not a competent forum for resolving such disputes" because conflicts about the "lawfulness of competing slates of presidential electors call for legal-type judgments rather than for raw exercises of political power."[166] He advised: "We should endeavor to keep Congress out of the picture, so far as that is possible to do. It is a large, unwieldy, undisciplined body (actually two bodies), unsuited in its structure, personnel and procedures to legal dispute resolution."[167]

His analysis is unpersuasive. *Bush* v. *Gore* had more to do with the Court's raw exercise of political power than "legal-type judgments." Further, Congress has long been a competent forum for resolving disputes about presidential elections. Both the Constitution and statutory law contemplate situations in which decisions about legislative and presidential elections are placed conclusively with Congress. Article I, Section 5, Clause 1, empowers each house of Congress to "be the Judge of the Elections, Returns and Qualifications of its own Members." Congress has rendered judgment on presidential elections in the past, including the Jefferson-Burr

---

165. David K. Ryden, "What Bush v. Gore Does and Does Not Tell Us About the Supreme Court and Electoral Politics," in The U.S. Supreme Court and the Electoral Process 251 (Ryden, ed., 2002).

166. Richard A. Posner, Breaking the Deadlock: The 2000 Election, the Constitution, and the Courts 145 (2001).

167. Id. at 250.

deadlock in 1800 and the Electoral Commission created by Congress in 1877 to resolve the Hayes-Tilden race. In 1824, electoral votes were divided among four candidates: Andrew Jackson, William Crawford, John Quincy Adams, and Henry Clay. The House picked Adams on the first ballot.[168]

Under the Electoral Count Act of 1887, reflected today in Sections 5 and 15 of Title 3, if states follow specified procedures their decisions are accepted by Congress when it meets to count electoral votes. Statutory procedures explain what happens in disputes over the counting of votes. The two houses, acting separately, need to concur on a series of questions. If they cannot concur, the matter goes to the House of Representatives, with each state having one vote.[169] Through these processes, statutory and constitutional, Congress appropriately makes "legal-type judgments."

Constitutional scholar Cass Sunstein agreed with Posner that the Court needed to decide *Bush* v. *Gore* because Congress was the wrong body to resolve the dispute. The Court's decision, according to Sunstein, "brought a chaotic situation to an abrupt end. From the standpoint of constitutional order, it is reasonable to speculate that any other conclusion would have been far worse. In all likelihood, the outcome would have been resolved in Congress, and here political partisanship might well have spiraled out of control."[170] In fact, there would have been no loss of control. The dispute would have gone to Congress, where a deadlock would have

---

168. Mary W. M. Hargreaves, The Presidency of John Quincy Adams 19–25, 36–40 (1988 ed.).

169. 3 U.S.C. § 15; U.S. Const., Amendment 12.

170. Cass R. Sunstein, "Order Without Law," 68 U. Chi. L. Rev. 757, 772–73 (2001).

occurred initially between the Republican House and the Democratic Senate.

Under established procedures, when the two chambers cannot concur, the matter goes to the House of Representatives. Because of Republican control over state delegations, the House would have selected Bush. His legitimacy under this procedure would have been far greater than under the Court's splintered and confused ruling. He would have been elected in accordance with existing law. In *Bush* v. *Gore,* the Court objected to standardless procedures in Florida while issuing a ruling that lacked credible and applicable standards. The *per curiam* opinion noted: "Our consideration is limited to the present circumstances."[171] In other words, whatever constitutional principles were at play on December 12, 2000, applied to that day only, and were not to be relied on or cited in the future.

25. Buckley v. Valeo. In a series of rulings, the Supreme Court has rejected statutory limits on campaign expenditures. The Court finds political speech, including by corporations, protected by the First Amendment. In competition with this judicial policy are concerns by Congress and state legislatures that the integrity, fairness, and public trust in elections should outweigh arguments for unrestrained campaign spending. In both *Buckley* (1976) and *Citizens United* (2010), the Court held that unlimited expenditures by corporations and labor unions in elections are constitutionally protected and may not be restricted by Congress. These judicial rulings rest largely on three court-made principles: (1) corporations are "persons," (2) money is "speech," and (3) corporate expenditures are "speech" protected by the First Amendment.

---

171. 531 U.S. at 109.

The judicial policy on campaign spending is rooted in the Court's decision in *Buckley*, which upheld a congressional limit on personal contributions but struck down a limit on independent expenditures.[172] The Court accepted the argument that contributions resemble *quid pro quo* and may invite political corruption. Although expenditures are not immune from corruption, the Court announced: "A restriction on the amount of money a person or group can spend on political communication during a campaign necessarily reduces the quantity of expression by restricting the number of issues discussed, the depth of their exploration, and the size of the audience reached."[173] More important to the Court than public trust in elections was what is defined as political speech under the First Amendment.

The ruling is difficult to comprehend because it was issued as a *per curiam* opinion for which no justice took responsibility. Justice Stevens did not participate. As noted by Ruth Bader Ginsburg when she served on the D.C. Circuit, judges generally do not labor over *per curiam* opinions "with the same intensity they devote to signed opinions."[174] *Per curiam* decisions are usually brief. The one in *Buckley* covers 138 pages, followed by an appendix of 91 pages with statutory language. Next comes 60 pages of remarks by five justices. Each one concurred with some parts of the *per curiam* but dissented from others.[175] The result: a confusing and incoherent mix that makes it difficult to count the votes.

---

172. Buckley v. Valeo, 424 U.S. 1 (1976).

173. Id. at 19.

174. Ruth Bader Ginsburg, "Remarks on Writing Separately," 65 Wash. L. Rev. 133, 139 (1990).

175. For the manner in which the per curiam in Buckley was drafted, see Richard L. Hasen, "The Untold Drafting History of Buckley v. Valeo," 2 Election Law J. 241 (2003).

Chief Justice Burger objected that the *per curiam*'s decision to dissect the statute "bit by bit, casting off vital parts," left a remainder he doubted was "workable."[176] He challenged the effort to distinguish between contributions and expenditures, upholding one but not the other. To him, contributions and expenditures "are two sides of the same First Amendment coin" and the *per curiam*'s analysis "will not wash."[177] In his judgment, the statute "as it now stands is unworkable and inequitable."[178] Justices White and Blackmun also rejected the *per curiam*'s distinction between contributions and expenditures.[179]

Attacks by Justices. From 1976 to the present, justices have been highly critical of *Buckley.* Strong objections came from both conservative and liberal justices, often for different reasons. A 1978 decision struck down a Massachusetts statute that prohibited corporations from making contributions or expenditures to referenda and elections. The Supreme Court split 5–4.[180] A dissent by White, joined by Brennan and Marshall, rejected the reasoning in *Buckley.* White observed that in the arena of campaign finance "the expertise of legislators is at its peak and that of judges is at its very lowest."[181] A separate dissent by Rehnquist objected that the Court should have deferred to the judgment of Massachusetts in protecting the integrity of its elections.[182] In 1981, the Court divided 5–4 in deciding how to interpret and apply *Buckley* with regard

---

176. Buckley v. Valeo, 424 U.S. at 235–36 (Burger, C.J., opinion).

177. Id. at 241, 244.

178. Id. at 252.

179. Id. at 259 (White, J., opinion); id. at 290 (Blackmun, J., opinion).

180. First National Bank of Boston v. Bellotti, 435 U.S. 765 (1978).

181. Id. at 804.

182. Id. at 823 (Rehnquist, J., dissenting).

to corporate and union contributions to a political committee.[183] A dissent by Stewart, joined by Burger, Powell, and Rehnquist, objected to the majority's reasoning.

The difficulty of finding agreement on campaign finance cases was evident in 1982 when an evenly divided Court affirmed the judgment of a lower court.[184] The Court managed to produce a unanimous ruling in 1982,[185] but divided once again in a 1985 case, with five justices deciding that a campaign finance provision violated the First Amendment and three (White, Brennan, and Marshall) deciding it did not.[186] Three dissenters regarded *Buckley* as "wrongly decided."[187] In 1986, five justices interpreted the distinction between contributions and expenditures one way; four justices in dissent saw the distinction the opposite way.[188] A 1990 Court decision produced a 6–3 decision on the meaning of *Buckley,* with Scalia, Kennedy, and O'Connor in dissent.[189] The decision in that case, *Austin,* upheld limits on expenditures by corporations but would be overruled in *Citizens United.*

In a campaign finance case in 1996, six justices dissented in part.[190] A decision in 2000 produced dissents from Kennedy,

183. California Medical Assn. v. FEC, 453 U.S. 182 (1981).

184. Common Cause v. Schmitt, 455 U.S. 129 (1982).

185. FEC v. National Right to Work Committee, 459 U.S. 197 (1982).

186. FEC v. National Conservative PAC, 470 U.S. 480 (1985).

187. Id. at 507.

188. FEC v. Massachusetts Citizens for Life, Inc., 479 U.S. 243, 270 (1986). Dissents by Chief Justice Rehnquist and Justices White, Blackmun, and Stevens.

189. Austin v. Michigan Chamber of Commerce, 494 U.S. 652 (1990).

190. Colorado Republican Federal Campaign Comm. v. Federal Election Comm'n, 518 U.S. 604 (1996) (Chief Justice Rehnquist and Justices Kennedy, Scalia, Thomas, Stevens, and Ginsburg).

Thomas, and Scalia. Kennedy, who later wrote for the Court in *Citizens United,* stated: "The plain fact is that the compromise the Court invented in *Buckley* set the stage for a new kind of speech to enter the political system."[191] That language is remarkable. Kennedy acknowledged that the Court in *Buckley* was not interpreting the Constitution. It was "inventing" something, as it did in *Plessy, Lochner, Curtiss-Wright,* and many other flawed and discredited decisions.

Kennedy suggested there were sufficient grounds "to reject *Buckley*'s wooden formula."[192] The "melancholy history of campaign finance in *Buckley*'s wake shows what can happen when we intervene in the dynamics of speech and expression by inventing an artificial scheme of our own."[193] Concluding that "*Buckley* has not worked,"[194] he added: "I would overrule *Buckley* and then free Congress or state legislatures to attempt some new reform, if, based upon their own considered view of the First Amendment, it is possible to do so."[195] A separate dissent by Thomas, joined by Scalia, similarly referred to "the analytic fallacies of our flawed decision in *Buckley* v. *Valeo*" and said, "our decision in *Buckley* was in error, and I would overrule it."[196] In 2001, the Court divided 5–4 on a campaign finance case.[197]

A campaign finance decision in 2003 consumed 272 pages, with seven justices dissenting in part: Scalia, Thomas,

---

191. Nixon v. Shrink Missouri Government PAC, 528 U.S. 377, 406 (2000) (Kennedy, J. dissenting).

192. Id. at 407.

193. Id.

194. Id. at 408.

195. Id. at 409–10.

196. Id. at 410.

197. Federal Election Comm'n v. Colorado Republican Federal Campaign Comm., 533 U.S. 431 (2001).

Kennedy, Rehnquist, Stevens, Ginsburg, and Breyer.[198] Thomas, joined by Scalia, spoke about "the errors of *Buckley*."[199] Despite chronic problems with *Buckley*, a plurality of the Court in 2006 relied on it to prevent Vermont from imposing limits on campaign expenditures.[200] The plurality depended in large part on *stare decisis* to avoid revisiting and rethinking *Buckley*. Thomas and Scalia rejected the plurality's approach, pointing to "the continuing inability of the Court (and the plurality here) to apply *Buckley* in a coherent and principled fashion."[201] To Stevens, dissenting, "*Buckley*'s holding on expenditure limits is wrong" and "the time has come to overrule it."[202]

A 2007 case found the Court once again divided 5–4, this time in holding unconstitutional a federal statute (the Bipartisan Campaign Reform Act, or BCRA) that made it a federal crime for any corporation to broadcast shortly before an election any communication that names a federal candidate for elected office and that is targeted for the electorate.[203] The Court's lineup was significant: five conservatives (Roberts, Scalia, Kennedy, Thomas, and Alito) arrayed against four liberal-moderates (Souter, Stevens, Ginsburg, and Breyer)—the same configuration that would decide *Citizens United* in 2010. In 2008, in striking down Arizona's effort to avoid corruption by creating a public financing system, the Court's alignment was basically unchanged from 2007:

198. McConnell v. Federal Election Comm'n, 540 U.S. 93 (2003).

199. Id. at 266.

200. Randall v. Sorrell, 548 U.S. 230 (2006).

201. Id. at 266.

202. Id. at 274.

203. Federal Election Comm'n v. Wisconsin Right to Life, 551 U.S. 449 (2007).

Roberts, Scalia, Kennedy, Thomas, and Alito against the Arizona law, and a new mix of liberal-moderates supporting it: Kagan, Ginsburg, Breyer, and Sotomayor.[204]

26. Citizens United. Two issues dominate the debate about limiting corporate expenditures in campaigns. First, are corporations "persons" entitled to the rights available to natural persons? If there is a difference, may Congress and the states regulate corporate expenditures in a manner that would be impermissible for citizens? Second, granted the importance of political participation in elections and democracy, does the right of "speech" extend equally and identically to corporations and individuals? Those questions are explored in the next two sections.

Are Corporations "Persons"? In *Dartmouth College* v. *Woodward* in 1819, Chief Justice Marshall explained that a corporation "is an artificial being, invisible, intangible, and existing only in contemplation of law. Being the mere creature of law, it possesses only those properties which the charter of its creation confers upon it, either expressly, or as incidental to its very existence."[205] Natural persons are not creatures of law. Of the properties conferred by legislatures on corporations, Marshall said: "Among the most important are immortality."[206] No such property extends to natural persons.

---

204. Arizona Free Enterprise Club's Freedom Club PAC v. Bennett, 564 U.S. ___ (2011). See also Davis v. Federal Election Commission, 554 U.S. 724 (2008).

205. Trustees of Dartmouth College v. Woodward, 17 (4 Wheat.) 518, 636 (1819).

206. Id.

The first Supreme Court suggestion that corporations are persons came in *Santa Clara Co.* v. *Southern Pacific Railroad* (1886). Before oral argument began, Chief Justice Morrison Waite told the parties: "The court does not wish to hear argument on the question whether the provision in the Fourteenth Amendment to the Constitution, which forbids a State to deny to any person within its jurisdiction the equal protection of the laws, applies to these corporations. We are all of opinion that it does."[207] Without any briefing by the parties and without oral argument, Waite announced his opinion on a fundamental constitutional issue.

The unanimous decision by Justice John Marshall Harlan in *Santa Clara* made no reference to corporations being persons. The court reporter (J. C. Bancroft Davis), aware of Waite's remark before oral argument, asked him whether it should be included in the "headnotes" that preface the decision. What is binding is a Court's decision, not its headnotes. At most, headnotes are a handy guide and nothing more. Waite replied that Davis properly understood his remarks but left it to Davis whether to say anything about it in the headnotes. Davis began the headnotes with this sentence: "The defendant Corporations are persons within the intent of the clause in section 1 of the Fourteenth Amendment to the Constitution of the United States, which forbids a State to deny to any person within its jurisdiction the equal protection of the laws."[208]

The Fourteenth Amendment does not call a corporation a person. It begins, "All persons *born or naturalized* in the

---

207. Santa Clara Co. v. South. Pac. Railroad, 118 U.S. 394, 396 (1886).

208. Id. at 394–95. For background on this headnote, see Jack Beatty, Age of Betrayal: The Triumph of Money in America, 1865–1900, at 110–11, 171–78 (2008 ed.).

United States." Clearly that refers to natural persons, not artificial creations like corporations. They are not born or naturalized. They do not result from the sexual union of a man and a woman. They are created by statute and can be modified or eliminated by statute.

The Supreme Court has made many false and misleading claims about *Santa Clara*. In a decision in 1896, Justice Harlan said it was "now settled" that corporations are persons under the Fourteenth Amendment, citing his own opinion in *Santa Clara*. Of course, his ruling did not say that.[209] In 1906, he corrected his error. Writing for a unanimous Court, he analyzed the rights conferred by the Fourteenth Amendment, including language in Section 1 that no state may deprive "any person of life, liberty, or property, without due process of law; nor deny to any person within its jurisdiction the equal protection of the laws." Harlan found no support for the argument that a statute, if enforced against a corporation, would be inconsistent with the liberty guaranteed by the Fourteenth Amendment: "The liberty referred to in that Amendment is the liberty of natural, not artificial persons."[210] A year later, a unanimous decision by Harlan said the Fourteenth Amendment applies to "natural, not artificial, persons."[211] Five years later, the Court denied that corporations can claim protection under the Fourteenth Amendment for privileges and immunities of citizens of the United States.[212]

In a dissent in 1938, Justice Black said he did not believe the word "person" in the Fourteenth Amendment includes

---

209. Covington &c. Turnpike Co. v. Sandford, 164 U.S. 578, 592 (1896).

210. Northwestern Life Ins. Co. v. Riggs, 203 U.S. 243, 255 (1906).

211. Western Turf Association v. Greenberg, 204 U.S. 359, 363 (1907).

212. Selover, Bates & Co. v. Walsh, 226 U.S. 112, 126 (1912).

corporations.[213] He then wrote, falsely, that the Court in *Santa Clara* "decided for the first time that the word 'person' in the Fourteenth Amendment did in some instances include corporations."[214] Nothing in *Santa Clara* "decided" anything about corporations being persons under the Fourteenth Amendment. Justice Rehnquist, in a dissent in a 1978 case, helped put the record straight. He pointed to Justice Harlan's opinion for a unanimous Court in 1906 that liberty under the Fourteenth Amendment is "the liberty of natural, not artificial persons."[215]

During reargument of *Citizens United* on September 9, 2009, Justice Ginsburg asked Ted Olson, representing Citizens United, a perfectly clear question: "Mr. Olson, are you taking the position that there is no difference in the First Amendment rights of an individual? A corporation, after all, is not endowed by its creator with inalienable rights. So is there any distinction that Congress could draw between corporations and natural human beings for purposes of campaign finance?"[216] Olson sidestepped her question by citing *New York Times Co.* v. *Sullivan* (1964), which had nothing to do with campaign finance or the authority of Congress to regulate spending in federal elections. It had to do with an Alabama law and the right of citizens to a free press. Neither the opinion for the Court in *Sullivan* nor the several concurrences made any mention of corporations being persons

213. Conn. General Co. v. Johnson, 303 U.S. 77, 85 (1938).

214. Id. at 87.

215. First National Bank of Boston v. Bellotti, 435 U.S. 765, 822 (1978).

216. Citizens United v. Federal Election Commission, oral argument, U.S. Supreme Court, No. 08–205, September 9, 2009, at 4.

under the Fourteenth Amendment.[217] In his dissent in *Citizens United,* Justice Stevens rejected the alleged parallel between corporations and natural persons (see Box 4.3).

Box 4.3

Comparing Corporations to Natural Persons

The conceit that corporations must be treated identically to natural persons in the political sphere is not only inaccurate but also inadequate to justify the Court's disposition of this case.

In the context of election to public office, the distinction between corporate and human speakers is significant. Although they make enormous contributions to our society, corporations are not actually members of it. They cannot vote or run for office....

... Unlike our colleagues, [the Framers] had little trouble distinguishing corporations from human beings, and when they constitutionalized the right to free speech in the First Amendment, it was the free speech of individual Americans that they had in mind....

It might also be added that corporations have no consciences, no beliefs, no feelings, no thoughts, no desires. Corporations help structure and facilitate the activities of human beings, to be sure, and their "personhood" often serves as a useful legal fiction. But they are not themselves members of "We the People" by whom and for whom our Constitution was established.

Source: Citizens United v. Federal Election Comm'n, 558 U.S. ___, ___, ___, ___ (2010) (Stevens, J., dissenting).

Corporate "Speech." In the 2007 Wisconsin decision, Chief Justice Roberts said the First Amendment "requires us to err on the side of protecting political speech rather than suppressing it." To the Court, political speech by corporations requires protection. Natural persons are entitled to

---

217. New York Times Co. v. Sullivan, 376 U.S. 254 (1964).

free speech protection, but on what grounds are artificial persons (corporations) similarly protected? What prohibits Congress from legislating restrictions on corporate expenditures? The First Amendment states that Congress "shall make no law ... abridging the freedom of speech," and yet Roberts acknowledges that the Court's jurisprudence "over the past 216 years has rejected an absolutist interpretation of those words."[218]

A dissent by Justice White in 1985, joined by Brennan and Marshall, explained that the First Amendment "protects the right to speak, not the right to spend, and limitations on the amount of money that can be spent are not the same as restrictions on spending."[219] A concurrence by Justice Breyer in 2000 noted that the decision to contribute money to a political campaign is "a matter of First Amendment concern— not because money *is* speech (it is not); but because it *enables* speech."[220] Do five conservative justices actually protect the First Amendment and free speech, or are their arguments popular rationales for promoting corporate power? There are reasonable grounds for believing the latter.[221] A book by Judge J. Harvie Wilkinson III in 2012 asked a key question.

---

218. Federal Election Comm'n v. Wisconsin Right to Life, Inc., 551 U.S. 449, 482 (2007).

219. FEC v. National Conservative PAC, 470 U.S. 480, 508 (1985).

220. Nixon v. Shrink Missouri Government PAC, 528 U.S. 377, 400 (2000) (emphases in original).

221. Adam Liptak, "Study Challenges Supreme Court's Image as Defender of Free Speech," New York Times, January 8, 2012, at 21; David Cole, "The Roberts Court vs. Free Speech," New York Review of Books, August 19, 2010, at 80–81.

Did the majority in *Citizens United* "befriend free speech or smother small voices?"[222]

In *Citizens United,* the Court offered several assertions without providing any evidence. Here is one claim: "We now conclude that independent expenditures, including those made by corporations, do not give rise to corruption or the appearance of corruption."[223] Based on actual data, experience, and findings, Congress and a number of states determined that corporate spending not only provides the appearance of corruption, but results in actual corruption in political campaigns. The Court gives little or no weight to those elected branch judgments. Here is another judicial assertion in *Citizens United* unaccompanied by corroborating evidence: "The appearance of [corporate] influence or access, furthermore, will not cause the electorate to lose faith in our democracy."[224] To be persuasive, courts needs to anchor their decisions on evidence and convincing reasoning. Pure assertions (by any branch of government) are hollow.

The framers adopted the Free Speech Clause in the First Amendment to protect natural persons, not artificial persons such as corporations. There is no capacity on the part of corporations to "speak." They have no vocabulary, capacity to think, or ability to construct a sentence, much less deliver it. Persons working for a corporation can speak.

---

222. J. Harvie Wilkinson III, Cosmic Constitutional Theory: Why Americans Are Losing Their Inalienable Right to Self-Governance 74 (2012).

223. Citizens United v. Federal Election Comm'n, 558 U.S. ___, ___ (2010).

224. Id. at ___.

The First Amendment does not prohibit the elected branches from limiting corporate spending in political campaigns. Some statements in *Citizens United* are non sequiturs: "The fact that a corporation, or any other speaker, is willing to spend money to try to persuade voters presupposes that the people have the ultimate influence over elected officials."[225] Corporations successful in electing a president, senators, and representatives have greater influence over elected officials than a voter. Corporations spend money to exert political influence and control.

The Supreme Court had an opportunity in 2012 to learn something about the link between corporate expenditures and campaign corruption. Montana experienced a century of "copper kings" and other mining interests largely controlling the state's politics through financial means.[226] It responded by enacting legislation that prohibits a corporation from making "an expenditure in connection with a candidate or a political party."[227] The law clearly collided with *Citizens United,* but the Montana Supreme Court upheld the state law. The U.S. Supreme Court could have taken the case, ordered briefs and oral argument, and had some of its assertions tested by actual evidence. Instead, it issued a short *per curiam* decision reversing the Supreme Court of Montana.[228] A dissent signed by four justices (Breyer, Ginsburg, Sotomayor, and Kagan) stated that *Citizens United* "should not bar the Montana Supreme Court's

225. Id. at ___.

226. Robert Barnes and Dan Eggen, "Justices Reject States Law, Uphold Citizens United Ruling," Washington Post, June 26, 2012, at A7.

227. Mont. Code Ann. §13-35-227(1) (2011).

228. American Tradition Partnership, Inc. v. Bullock, 567 U.S. ___ (2012).

finding, made on the record before it, that independent expenditures by corporations did in fact lead to corruption or the appearance of corruption in Montana."[229]

This record underscores the pattern in earlier cases. When the Supreme Court in 2006 struck down Vermont's effort to curb campaign spending, Justices Souter, Ginsburg, and Stevens said the state had asked the Court to "determine whether its evidence" supported "a need to slow the fundraising treadmill."[230] They continued: "Three decades of experience since *Buckley* have taught us much, and the findings made by the Vermont Legislature on the pernicious effect of the nonstop pursuit of money are significant."[231]

Critics of *Citizens United* suggest two remedies: the Court could confess error or Congress and the states could ratify a constitutional amendment to reverse *Citizens United* and empower legislative action to regulate campaign expenditures. There is a third, and more plausible, alternative. In the field of campaign finance, the Court stands on shaky ground by relying on two judicial creations: corporations are "persons" and money is "speech." Congress should hold hearings and invite expert testimony on the damaging and corrupting influence of money on democratic government. Instead of trying to reconcile the confused and conflicting cases on campaign finance, Congress should start from scratch to produce a coherent, principled, evidence-based, and constructive law to protect democratic government.[232]

---

229. Id. at ___.

230. Randall v. Sorrell, 548 U.S. at 283.

231. Id.

232. Louis Fisher, "Saying What the Law Is: On Campaign Finance, It's Not Just for the Court; Congress Has a Co-Equal Say," National Law Journal, February 22, 2010, at 38.

The Court could declare the statute contrary to its rulings and therefore invalid, but it would be institutionally foolish to strike down a statute merely because it is incompatible with evidence-free Court rulings. The Court would show better judgment to say: "Congress has assembled evidence that was not available to us when we decided *Buckley* and *Citizens United.* We now, after due consideration, defer to the legislative judgment and overrule our decisions." If that were to happen, the Court would be under appropriate pressure to adopt a more deferential attitude toward state efforts to control campaign expenditures.

This and the preceding chapter analyzed judicial rulings that damaged the Supreme Court and the country. In some cases, the Court acknowledges the deficiency of an earlier decision and overrules it. On other occasions, as with *Korematsu,* a case is not overruled even when widely condemned for its reasoning and consequences.[233] A decision like *Citizens United* may be too recent to be overruled, but much of the legal community and the country has rejected its central tenets. It may be only a matter of time before the Court disowns much of it, particularly if the Court's composition changes to add another justice ready to reverse it. Chapter Five looks more broadly at the constitutional dialogues that involve all three branches. Frequently the final voice in protecting constitutional rights and liberties is not the Court, but the elected branches and the general public.

---

233. On May 20, 2011, Acting Solicitor General Neal Katyal pointed out that the Solicitor General in *Korematsu* failed to inform the Court of evidence that undermined the rationale for internment. Neal Katyal, "Confession of Error: The Solicitor General's Mistakes During the Japanese-American Internment Cases," May 20, 2011; http://blogs.justice.gov/main/archives/1346. Accessed Feb. 19, 2013.

CHAPTER FIVE
INDIVIDUAL AND MINORITY RIGHTS

Several decisions by the Supreme Court after the Civil War damaged the Court's reputation as guardian of individual and private rights. Citizens sought protection from the courts only to lose on a regular basis. Gradually they learned their interests were better defended by legislative bodies at the state and national levels. When Congress passed legislation in 1875 to provide blacks with equal access to public accommodations, the Supreme Court declared the legislation unconstitutional. Women who wanted to practice law found that the legislative branch, not the courts, would protect their interests. In 1896, the Court granted its blessing to a "separate but equal" statute passed in Louisiana to require blacks and whites to sit separately in railroad cars. These judicial errors survived until the 1950s and 1960s, when they were finally reversed by the Court's desegregation decision in 1954 and the Civil Rights Act of 1964. Congress has frequently been a better defender of religious liberty than the courts.

Protecting the Rights of Women

After the Civil War, women began to attend medical and law schools and pursue other professional opportunities formerly dominated by men. They found legal support from legislative bodies, but not from courts. The theory of British legal scholar William Blackstone, writing in the late 1700s, placed women in a subordinate status. He wrote about the doctrine of "coverture," which in marriage made husband and wife "one person in law: that is, the very being or legal existence of the woman is suspended during the marriage, or at least is incorporated and consolidated into that of the husband: under whose wing, protection, and *cover,* she performs every thing."[1] Although some women did not marry and should not have subjected to his doctrine, courts treated unmarried women as the exception, not the rule.

After studying law, Myra Bradwell applied for admission to the Illinois bar in 1869. She needed the approval of an all-male panel of judges to practice in Illinois. They rejected her application solely on the ground that she was a woman. Her appeal to the Supreme Court of Illinois failed.[2] Of her qualifications the court said: "We have no doubt."[3] British law and custom weighed heavily in the court's analysis, however. Female attorneys "were unknown in England, and a proposition that a woman should enter the courts of Westminster Hall in that capacity, or as a barrister, would have created hardly

---

1. 2 William Blackstone, Commentaries on the Laws of England *442 (1783) (emphasis in original).

2. In re Bradwell, 55 Ill. 535 (1869).

3. Id. at 536.

less astonishment than one that she should ascend the bench of Bishops, or be elected to a seat in the House of Commons."[4]

If British customs seemed insufficient to block the professional advancement of women, the Illinois court had no difficulty in discovering much higher authority: "That God designed the sexes to occupy different spheres of action, and that it belonged to men to make, apply and execute the laws, was regarded as an almost axiomatic truth."[5] This type of judicial reasoning was common. Given these rigidities in the courts, women were more likely to find success appealing to legislative bodies. The Illinois court concluded that if change was needed, "let it be made by that department of the government to which the constitution has entrusted the power of changing the laws."[6] A legislative body could decide if allowing women to "engage in the hot strifes of the bar, in the presence of the public, and with momentous verdicts the prizes of the struggle, would not tend to destroy the deference and delicacy with which it is the pride of our ruder sex to treat her."[7]

Bradwell took the judicial hint and sought assistance from the Illinois legislature. In 1872 it passed a bill stating that no person "shall be precluded or debarred from any occupation, profession or employment (except military) on account of sex."[8] The statute added some qualifications. Nothing in it was to be construed "as requiring any female to work on

---

4. Id. at 539.

5. Id.

6. Id. at 540.

7. Id. at 542.

8. Illinois Laws, 1871–1972, at 578.

streets or roads, or serve on juries."[9] Progress would come one step at a time.

Following this action by the state legislature, Bradwell took her case to the U.S. Supreme Court, hoping to establish a national right for women to practice law under the Privileges and Immunities Clause of the Fourteenth Amendment. Courts hear a case argued by opposing parties, but in Bradwell's case, after her attorney presented his argument, the court record states: "No opposing counsel."[10] In a brief opinion, the Court denied that the right of women to practice law in the courts was a privilege belonging to citizens of the United States.[11] A concurrence by Justice Joseph P. Bradley relied on Blackstone's doctrine of coverture, insisting that man "is, or should be, woman's protector and defender."[12] The "natural and proper timidity and delicacy" of women made them "unfit" for many occupations.[13] A "divine ordinance" commanded that a woman's primary mission in life is to the home. While many women did not marry, a general rule imposed upon females the "paramount destiny and mission" to fulfill the roles of wife and mother. "This is the law of the Creator."[14]

Attorney Belva Lockwood, aware that the U.S. Supreme Court had adopted a rule prohibiting women from practicing there, went to Congress for support. She drafted language and worked closely with lawmakers to overturn the Court's rule.

---

9. Id.

10. Bradwell v. State, 83 U.S. (16 Wall.) 130, 137 (1883).

11. Id. at 139.

12. Id. at 141.

13. Id.

14. Id.

Her bill provided that when any woman had been admitted to the bar of the highest court of a state, or of the supreme court of the District of Columbia, and was otherwise qualified as set forth in the bill (three years of practice and a person of good moral character, as with male attorneys), she may be admitted to practice before the U.S. Supreme Court.[15] Working in a Congress with all male members, her bill became law within one year.

The bill reached the House floor on February 21, 1878, and passed by a vote of 169 to 87.[16] The bill encountered delays in the Senate, but Senator Aaron Sargent of California pushed hard for passage. His appeal looked to future opportunities, not to the doctrines of Blackstone and British precedents (see Box 5.1).

Box 5.1

Congressional Support for the Rights of Women

I say again, men have not the right, in contradiction to the intentions, the wishes, the ambitions, of women, to say that their sphere shall be circumscribed, that bounds shall be set which they cannot pass. The enjoyment of liberty, the pursuit of happiness in her own way, is as much the birthright of woman as of man. In this land man has ceased to dominate over his fellow [male slaves]—let him cease to dominate over his sister; for he has no higher right to do the latter than the former. It is mere oppression to say to the bread-seeking woman, you shall labor only in certain narrow ways for your living, we will hedge you out by law from profitable employments, and monopolize them for ourselves.

Source: 8 Cong. Rec. 1084 (1879).

---

15. 7 Cong. Rec. 1235 (1878).
16. Id.

The Senate passed the bill, 39 to 20, and it became law.[17] Within two years of *Bradwell* the Supreme Court delivered another setback to the rights of women. A unanimous Court agreed that women are citizens but denied that the Fourteenth Amendment added substantive rights to previous privileges and immunities. As interpreted by the Court, the amendment limited voting to men. It reasoned that the Fifteenth Amendment gave blacks the right to vote. No such right was conferred to women. It held that women, like children, were "citizens" and "persons" in the constitutional sense, but such status did not automatically bring with it the right to vote.[18]

Judicial attitudes about the rights of women remained in the age of Blackstone. In 1948, the Supreme Court upheld a Michigan law that prohibited female bartenders unless they were the wife or daughter of the male owner. Divided 6 to 3, the Court decided that the law did not violate the Equal Protection Clause of the Fourteenth Amendment.[19] Writing for the majority, Justice Felix Frankfurter began with smug assurance: "Beguiling as the subject is, it need not detain us for long. To ask whether or not the Equal Protection of the Laws Clause of the Fourteenth Amendment barred Michigan from making the classification the State has made between wives and daughters of non-owners, is one of those rare instances where to state the question is in effect to answer it."[20] Three dissenters, finding the case far more complicated, concluded that the state had arbitrarily discriminated between men and women.

---

17. Id.; 20 Stat. 292 (1879).
18. Minor v. Happensett, 88 U.S. (21 Wall.) 162 (1875).
19. Goeseart v. Cleary, 335 U.S. 464 (1948).
20. Id. at 465.

Traditional attitudes toward women continued to flavor judicial rulings. A unanimous Court in 1966 agreed that women could be largely exempted from jury service because they are "still regarded as the center of home and family life."[21] Remnants of the law of coverture survived as late as 1966.[22] It was not until 1971 that the Supreme Court issued an opinion striking down an instance of sex discrimination. A unanimous Court declared invalid an Idaho law that preferred men over women in administering estates.[23] A study published that year denounced the failure of courts to defend the rights of women: "Our conclusion, independently reached, but completely shared, is that by and large the performance of American judges in the area of sex discrimination can be succinctly described as ranging from poor to abominable."[24]

Equal Accommodation for Blacks

In the same manner that the Supreme Court blocked the rights of women, so did it obstruct congressional efforts after the Civil War to extend rights to blacks. In 1875, Congress passed legislation to close the gap between the Declaration of Independence's "all men are created equal" and the Constitution. The preamble to the statute read: "Whereas, it is essential to just government we recognize the equality of all

---

21. Hoyt v. Florida, 368 U.S. 57, 62 (1961).

22. United States v. Yazell, 382 U.S. 341 (1966).

23. Reed v. Reed, 404 U.S. 71 (1971).

24. John D. Johnson, Jr. & Charles L. Knapp, "Sex Discrimination by Law: A Study in Judicial Perspective," 46 N.Y.U. L. Rev. 675, 676 (1971).

men before the law."[25] Although the Civil War amendments formally elevated blacks to the status of citizen, in many states they were denied access to public facilities. Under the 1875 statute, all persons in the United States were entitled to the "full and equal enjoyment of the accommodations, advantages, facilities, and privileges of inns, public conveyances [transportation] on land and water, theaters, and other places of public amusement."[26]

Congress did not indicate the provision in the Constitution on which it relied. Because the Thirteenth Amendment abolished slavery, it could be argued that denying blacks access to public accommodations represented a "badge of slavery." The Fourteenth Amendment offered another possible source of constitutional authority. It provides that no state "shall make or enforce any law which shall abridge the privileges or immunities of citizens of the United States; nor shall any State deprive any person of life, liberty, or property, without due process of law; nor deny to any person within its jurisdiction the equal protection of the laws."[27]

In the House, Benjamin Butler of Massachusetts and chair of the Judiciary Committee rejected the charge that Congress was attempting to impose a national standard of "social equality" among blacks and whites. The issue, instead, was one of law: "The colored men are either American citizens or they are not. The Constitution, for good or evil, for right or for wrong, has made them American citizens; and the moment they were clothed with that attribute of citizenship, they stood on a political and legal equality with every other

---

25. 18 Stat. 335 (1875).

26. Id. at 336.

27. U.S. Const., amend. XIV, section 1.

citizen, be he whom he may."[28] Social equality, he explained, has nothing to do with law. Everyone has the right to freely select friends and associates. Those choices have nothing to do with access to public accommodations or to decide who someone sits next to in a theater or restaurant, or on a train. He acknowledged that he preferred not to sit next to some whites at public accommodations, but they had a right to be there.[29] Butler said the bill had nothing to do with social equality or with whites refusing to associate with blacks (see Box 5.2).

The bill passed the House 161 to 79 and the Senate 38 to 26.[30] President Ulysses S. Grant had some concerns about the bill, particularly a provision on equal access to schools.[31]

Box 5.2

Social Rights versus Legal Rights

There is not a white man at the South that would not associate with the negro—all that is required by this bill—if that negro were his servant. He would eat with him, suckle from her, play with her or him as children, be together with them in every way, provided they were slaves. There never has been an objection to such an association. But the moment that you elevate this black man to citizenship from a slave, then immediately he becomes offensive. That is why I say that this prejudice is foolish, unjust, illogical, and ungentlemanly.

Source: 3 Cong. Rec. 940 (1875).

---

28. 3 Cong. Rec. 939–40 (1875).

29. Id. at 940.

30. Id. at 991, 1870.

31. Bertram Wyatt-Brown, "The Civil Rights Act of 1875," 18 West. Pol. Q. 763, 773 (1965).

After that language was stripped from the bill, he signed it into law.[32]

The public accommodations law, challenged in five states (California, Kansas, Missouri, New York, and Tennessee), did not reach the Supreme Court until 1882. The following year, in the *Civil Rights Cases,* the Court struck down the public accommodation provision as a federal encroachment on the states and an interference with private relationships.[33] It found no basis in the Fourteenth Amendment for Congress to pass the legislation. Although the amendment empowers Congress to enact "by appropriate legislation" whatever is required to enforce the language, the Court ruled that Congress could regulate only "state action," not discrimination by private parties.[34] The Court suggested that Congress might have acted under its commerce power, especially in regulating "public conveyances passing from one State to another,"[35] but Congress did not invoke that authority and the question was not before the Court. As to the Thirteenth Amendment and its prohibition of slavery, the Court rejected the argument that denying persons access to public accommodations amounted to "servitude" or a "badge of slavery."[36]

Only one justice dissented, but it is perhaps the finest dissent ever written. With close analysis, Justice John Marshall Harlan regarded the Court's opinion as "entirely too narrow and artificial."[37] He noted that the Civil War Amendments were "adopted in the interest of liberty" and to

---

32. 18 Stat. 335 (1875).

33. 109 U.S. 3 (1883).

34. Id. at 11.

35. Id. at 19.

36. Id. at 20–25.

37. Id. at 26.

secure through congressional legislation "rights inhering in a state of freedom and belonging to American citizenship." The Court's interpretation defeated "the ends the people desired to accomplish, which they attempted to accomplish, and which they supposed they had accomplished by changes in their fundamental law."[38]

Harlan explained that the first section of the 1875 statute "was to prevent *race* discrimination in respect of the accommodations and facilities of inns, public conveyances, and places of public amusement."[39] As to the Thirteenth Amendment, he said it did "something more than to prohibit slavery as an *institution*."[40] States that had previously accepted slavery and fought a civil war to keep it should not be "left free, so far as national interference was concerned, to make or allow discrimination against that race, as such, in the enjoyment of those fundamental rights which by universal concession, inhere in a state of freedom."[41]

In analyzing the difference between state action and private discrimination, Justice Harlan reviewed precedents established for public conveyances on land and water. States created railroads as public highways for public use. Even if controlled and owned by private corporations, railroads functioned as public highways for the convenience of the public. Railroads acquired new territory because states seized land through the power of eminent domain. States regulated railroads by enacting speed and safety standards.[42]

---

38. Id.
39. Id. (emphasis in original).
40. Id. at 34 (emphasis in original).
41. Id.
42. Id. at 38–39.

With regards to inns and taverns, Harlan acknowledged that private owners built them without the state assistance given to railroads. But an innkeeper offered lodging to travelers seeking shelter for the night. Under laws existing for centuries, it was an innkeeper's duty to take all travelers and offer them room and food. An innkeeper had no legal right to accept one traveler and reject another. The innkeeper functioned as a public servant. If travelers could pay and rooms were available, an innkeeper could not exclude them.[43]

What of places of public amusement? They received no state assistance, as railroads did, and there was no issue of needing shelter or food for the night as in the case of inns. But places of public amusement, including theaters, were not purely private establishments. They were established and licensed by public officials.[44] In case of racial discrimination, what type of court could the individual turn to? State or federal? The 1875 statute required it be federal courts. Harlan concluded that racial discrimination by places of public accommodation constituted a badge of servitude that Congress could regulate through the Thirteenth Amendment.[45] All three Civil War Amendments ended with this language: Congress shall have power to enforce the amendments "by appropriate legislation." It was for Congress, Harlan said, "not the judiciary, to say that legislation is appropriate—that is—best adapted to the end to be attained."[46]

---

43. Id. at 40–41.
44. Id. at 41.
45. Id. at 43.
46. Id. at 51.

What Congress attempted to do in 1875 with respect to public accommodations finally prevailed almost a century later. Federal courts began to follow Harlan's understanding of the relationship between "state action" and private parties, enabling government to act against racial discrimination. A restaurant in a building owned by the state of Delaware refused to serve blacks. The building had been constructed with public funds for public purposes and was owned and operated by the state. Part of the building was leased to a privately owned restaurant, but the Supreme Court in 1961 held that the state jointly operated the restaurant and any racial exclusion violated the Fourteenth Amendment.[47]

Congress included in the Civil Rights Act of 1964 a section on public accommodations, relying on both the Fourteenth Amendment and the commerce power.[48] The bill passed with top-heavy majorities of 289–126 in the House and 73–27 in the Senate. Private groups lobbied for the bill, creating a political base that helped educate citizens and build public support. The rights of blacks were secured far better through this majoritarian process than through judicial action. In two unanimous decisions, the Court relied on the commerce power to uphold the public accommodation law.[49] The active, reliable judgment in protecting constitutional rights of minorities came from the elected branches, finally overcoming judicial obstruction.

---

47. Burton v. Wilmington Pkg. Auth., 365 U.S. 715 (1961).

48. S. Rept. No. 872, 88th Cong., 2d Sess. 12–14 (1964); H. Rept. No. 914, 88th Cong., 1st Sess. 2–3, 20–22, 98–101 (1963); H. Rept. No. 914 (Part 2), 88th Cong., 1st Sess. 1–2, 7–9 (1963).

49. Heart of Atlanta Motel v. United States, 379 U.S. 241, 250 (1964); Katzenbach v. McClung, 379 U.S. 294 (1964).

Court-Made Doctrine: "Separate but Equal"

From 1865 to the *Civil Rights Cases* of 1883, the Supreme Court issued a number of decisions that weakened the promise and commitment of the Thirteenth, Fourteenth, and Fifteenth Amendments. The *Slaughter-House Cases* of 1873 expressed strong judicial support for independent state powers. The majority rejected interpretations of the Civil War Amendments that would "fetter and degrade the State governments by subjecting them to the control of Congress."[50] In *United States* v. *Cruikshank* (1876), the Court promoted the doctrine of "dual federalism," attempting to establish a pure separation between federal and state powers: "The powers which one possesses, the other does not."[51] Under that theory, state sovereignty could prevail over national powers exercised through the Civil War Amendments. The protection of due process and equal protection would be left to the states.[52]

Part of the Civil Rights Act of 1875 granted rights to jurors in federal and state courts. No citizen qualified to serve could be disqualified "on account of race, color, or previous condition of servitude."[53] A state judge in Virginia violated the provision and was prosecuted in federal court. In *Ex parte Virginia* (1880), the Supreme Court upheld the statutory provision and gave a broad reading to the Thirteenth and Fourteenth Amendments.[54] The objective of the statute and the amendments was to "raise the colored race from that

---

50. 83 U.S. (16 Wall.) 36, 78 (1873).
51. 92 U.S. (2 Otto.) 542, 550 (1876).
52. Id. at 554–55.
53. 18 Stat. 336, sec. 4 (1875).
54. 100 U.S. 339 (1880).

condition of inferiority and servitude in which most of them had previously stood, into perfect equality of civil rights with all other persons within the jurisdiction of the States."[55] The amendments were intended "to take away all possibility of oppression by law because of race or color. They were intended to be, what they really are, limitations of the power of the States and enlargements of the power of Congress."[56] To the Court, the amendments worked a fundamental change in the relationship between the national government and the states. It did not matter that the congressional relationship was "restrictive of what the State might have done before the constitutional amendment was adopted," and any enforcement by Congress was "no invasion of State sovereignty."[57]

Yet three years later, with the *Civil Rights Cases*, the Court decided to swing in a fundamentally different direction to read the Fourteenth Amendment narrowly in applying it to state and private action. The issue in *Ex parte Virginia* of racial discrimination in the selection of jurors appeared to be of a different, and less threatening, character than giving blacks equal access to public accommodations. The decision in the *Civil Rights Cases* provided the legal orientation used by the Court when it dealt with Louisiana's "separate but equal" doctrine in *Plessy* v. *Ferguson* (1896).

In the years following the Civil War, there was no clear pattern in the South in segregating blacks and whites in transportation systems. Blacks and whites sometimes traveled in the same railroad car. Southern transportation "was not rigidly segregated in the quarter-century after the Civil

---

55. Id. at 344–45.
56. Id. at 345.
57. Id. at 346.

War."[58] By the late 1880s, many Southern states began passing Jim Crow transportation laws to separate blacks and whites.[59] The timing here is significant. This movement came after the Supreme Court, in the *Civil Rights Cases*, invalidated the equal accommodations statute passed by Congress. Through that decisive step the Court opened the door to the "separate but equal" doctrine in public accommodations, which would have been impermissible under congressional policy.

In *Plessy,* the Court divided 7 to 1 in upholding a Louisiana statute enacted in 1890. The law required railway companies to provide equal but separate accommodations for white and black passengers, either by having two or more coaches for each train or by dividing a coach with a partition between the two races. For passengers who insisted on going into a coach or compartment where they did not belong, the state could impose fines or imprisonment. Louisiana's policy, said the Court, did not conflict with the Thirteenth or Fourteenth Amendment.[60] The statute made one exception. It did not apply "to nurses attending children of the other race."[61]

An issue in *Plessy* was the capacity of train officials to distinguish between white and black passengers. The petitioner in the case, Homer Plessy, was "seven eighths Caucasian and one eighth African blood."[62] At what point could the state find it impossible (or highly arbitrary) to determine if someone of mixed descent belonged to one race or the other? The

---

58. Charles A. Lofgren, The Plessy Case: A Legal-Historical Interpretation 9 (1987). See also id. at 11–13.

59. Id. at 21.

60. Plessy v. Ferguson, 163 U.S. 537 (1896).

61. Id. at 541.

62. Id. at 538.

conductor ordered Plessy to leave the white coach and move to a black coach. When he refused, a police officer removed him and he was imprisoned.[63]

Justice Henry Billings Brown wrote for the majority. Turning first to the Thirteenth Amendment and its prohibition of slavery and involuntary servitude (except for conviction of a crime), he regarded the lack of conflict between the state law and the constitutional amendment as "too clear for argument."[64] He reached that conclusion by citing the judgment in the *Civil Rights Cases* that refused blacks equal accommodation to public facilities, including railroads. Such restrictions, he said, "cannot be justly regarded as imposing any badge of slavery or servitude."[65] Had the Court in the *Civil Rights Cases* not invalidated the congressional statute of 1875, Brown could not so easily have dismissed the Thirteenth Amendment issue. The Court was building not on constitutional provisions and their intent but rather on its own interpretation or misinterpretation.

Justice Brown added: "A statute which implies merely a legal distinction between the white and colored races—a distinction which is founded in the color of the two races, and which must always exist so long as white men are distinguished from the other race by color—has no tendency to destroy the legal equality of the two races, or reestablish a state of involuntary servitude."[66] Would he have made that statement had Louisiana distinguished whites from other races, including Hispanics and Asians, or perhaps on the

---

63. Id.
64. Id. at 542.
65. Id.
66. Id. at 543.

basis of national origin, distinguishing French stock from non-French stock?

With regard to the Fourteenth Amendment, Justice Brown sought guidance from the *Slaughter-House Cases* of 1873, which greatly undermined the national authority announced in the Civil War Amendments and instead gave added protection to independent state rights.[67] Oddly, Brown wrote this about the Fourteenth Amendment: "The object of the amendment was undoubtedly to enforce the absolute equality of the two races before the law, but in the nature of things it could not have been intended to abolish distinctions based upon color, or to enforce social, as distinguished from political equality, or a commingling of the two races upon terms unsatisfactory to either."[68] If the purpose of the amendment was to enforce absolute equality of the two races before the law, it should prohibit "separate but equal" legislation. The issue was never a question of "commingling" the two races, but rather of establishing political—not social—equality.

Brown continued: "Laws permitting, and even requiring, their separation in places where they are liable to be brought into contact do not necessarily imply the inferiority of either race to the other, and have been generally, if not universally, recognized as within the competency of the state legislatures in the exercise of their police power."[69] First, passage of the law by a white Louisiana legislature clearly implied that blacks were inferior to whites, and that whites did not want to be in the company of blacks. Second, Brown's reasoning would support Nazi Germany's policy of separating Jews and Gentiles,

---

67. Id.
68. Id. at 544.
69. Id.

all ostensibly to exercise the police power. Jews understood that the state regarded them as inferior.

An additional point by Justice Brown: "The most common instance of this is connected with the establishment of separate schools for white and colored children, which has been held to be a valid exercise of the legislative power even by courts of States where the political rights of the colored race have been longest and most earnestly enforced."[70] The issue of school segregation had no application to the Louisiana railroad law. Brown spent more than a page discussing state decisions to provide for separate schools for blacks and whites, including in his home state of Massachusetts.[71] He even cited laws forbidding interracial marriage, which had no relevance to the case before him.[72]

To Justice Brown, it was a question "whether the statute of Louisiana is a reasonable regulation, and with respect to this there must necessarily be a large discretion on the part of the legislature."[73] The Court extended no such deference to Congress when it passed the Civil Rights Act of 1875. Interestingly, Brown did defer to Congress when it passed legislation "requiring separate schools for colored children in the District of Columbia, the constitutionality of which does not seem to have been questioned, or the corresponding acts of state legislatures."[74]

In conclusion, Justice Brown considered "the underlying fallacy of the plaintiff's argument to consist in the assumption

---

70. Id.
71. Id. at 544–45.
72. Id. at 545.
73. Id. at 550.
74. Id. at 551.

that the enforced separation of the two races stamps the colored race with a badge of inferiority. If this be so, it is not by reason of anything found in the act, but solely because the colored race chooses to put that construction upon it."[75] What other construction could blacks place upon the Louisiana statute? The state did not consider it necessary to exclude other races or any nationalities or religions from the presence of whites. Brown, generally regarded as "a centrist" who always sought "the middle ground,"[76] was determined to go to the edge in this case. He offered this thought: if blacks became the "dominant power" in the state legislature and enacted a law separating blacks and whites in railroad cars, whites would not assume their race was placed in "an inferior position."[77] Still further: "If one race be inferior to the other socially, the Constitution of the United States cannot put them upon the same plane."[78] The case had nothing to do with social equality. It had to do with equal access to public railways.

As with the *Civil Rights Cases,* Justice Harlan was the sole dissenter. He pointed out that no one disputed that a railroad "is a public highway" and that the corporation who owns and operates it exercises a public function.[79] With regard to Justice Brown's belief that the Louisiana law did not discriminate against either race, but merely prescribed a rule applicable equally to whites and blacks, Harlan countered: "Every one

---

75. Id.

76. Congressional Quarterly's Guide to the U.S. Supreme Court 831 (1979).

77. 163 U.S. at 551.

78. Id. at 552.

79. Id.

knows that the statute in question had its origin in the purpose, not so much to exclude white persons from railroad cars occupied by blacks, as to exclude colored persons from coaches occupied by or assigned to white persons."[80]

Although to Justice Harlan the white race in America was dominant in terms of "prestige, in achievements, in education, in wealth and in power," in view of the Constitution and "the eye of the law," there was no superior or dominant ruling class.[81] "There is no caste here. Our Constitution is color-blind, and neither knows nor tolerates classes among citizens. In respect of all civil rights, all citizens are equal before the law."[82] He predicted that *Plessy* would "prove to be quite as pernicious as the decision made by this tribunal in the *Dred Scott case*."[83] A passage in Harlan's dissent shows that he was color-blind as to whites and blacks, but not to the Chinese:

> There is a race so different from our own that we do not permit those belonging to it to become citizens of the United States. Persons belonging to it are, with few exceptions, absolutely excluded from our country. I allude to the Chinese race. But by the statute in question, a Chinaman can ride in the same passenger coach with white citizens of the United States, while citizens

---

80. Id. at 557.

81. Id. at 559.

82. Id.

83. Id. For analyses on Plessy: Cheryl I. Harris, "The Story of Plessy v. Ferguson: The Death and Resurrection of Racial Formalism," in Constitutional Law Stories (Michael C. Dorf, ed., 2004), and Paul Oberst, "The Strange Career of Plessy v. Ferguson," 15 Ariz. L. Rev. 389 (1975).

of the black race in Louisiana, many of whom, perhaps, risked their lives for the preservation of the Union, who are entitled, by law, to participate in the political control of the State and nation, who are not excluded, by law or by reason of their race, from public stations of any kind, and who have all the legal rights that belong to white citizens, are yet declared to be criminals, liable to imprisonment, if they ride in a public coach occupied by citizens of the white race.[84]

Articles that praise Justice Harlan for his principled dissent in *Plessy* overlook his inconsistent statements on the Chinese. In a 1994 article, constitutional scholar Cass Sunstein referred to Harlan's dissent and said he wrote "one of the greatest sentences in American law: 'There is no caste here.'"[85] For Harlan, there was no caste between white and black. There was for the Chinese. Political scientist Henry J. Abraham, in a tribute to Harlan in 1955, highlights this sentence from *Plessy*: "Our Constitution is color-blind, and neither knows nor tolerates classes among citizens."[86] Abraham said that Harlan's concerns for blacks "echoed for other minorities as well, such as the Chinese,"[87] but did not comment on Harlan's reference to the Chinese in *Plessy*.

---

84. 163 U.S. at 561. For Harlan's position on the Chinese: Gabriel J. Chin, "The Plessy Myth: Justice Harlan and the Chinese Cases," 82 Iowa L. Rev. 151 (1996).

85. Cass Sunstein, "The Anticaste Principle," 92 Mich. L. Rev. 2410, 2435 (1994), citing Plessy v. Ferguson, 163 U.S. at 559.

86. Henry J. Abraham, "John Marshall Harlan: A Justice Neglected," 41 Va. L. Rev. 871, 871 (1955).

87. Id. at 880.

Compulsory Flag Salutes

In 1940, a commanding 8–1 majority of the Supreme Court upheld a compulsory flag salute in Pennsylvania that forced children to violate their religious beliefs. So defective and unpersuasive was the opinion and so swift the public condemnation that within three years the Court reversed itself. The Jehovah's Witness parents of two children objected that the flag salute violated their interpretation of the biblical provision in Exodus 20:4–5: "Thou shalt not make unto thee any graven image, or any likeness of any thing that is in heaven above, or that is in the earth beneath, or that is in the water under the earth. Thou shalt not bow down thyself to them, nor serve under them."

In 1937, a federal district judge found the statute to be unconstitutional. The case involved two children, Lillian Gobitas (age thirteen) and her brother William (twelve). (The family name, incorrectly spelled "Gobitis" early in the litigation, remained misspelled at every stage thereafter.[88]) School authorities concluded that their refusal to salute the flag constituted an act of insubordination that required expulsion from the public school. To the federal judge, the state could not violate religious beliefs unless it could demonstrate it necessary for the public safety, health, morals, property, or personal rights.[89] The Pennsylvania constitution, drawing from the history of religious freedom in the state, provided that "all men have a natural and indefeasible right

---

88. Shawn Francis Peters, Judging Jehovah's Witnesses: Religious Persecution and the Dawn of the Rights Revolution 19 (2000).

89. Gobitis v. Minersville School Dist., 21 F.Supp. 581, 584 (E.D. Pa. 1937).

to worship Almighty God according to the dictates of their own consciences; ... no human authority can, in any case whatever, control or interfere with the rights of conscience." The judge pointed to religious intolerance that was "again rearing its ugly head in other parts of the world," including anti-Semitism in Nazi Germany.[90] The Third Circuit upheld his decision, finding it difficult to see "the essential relationship between infant patriotism and the martial spirit."[91]

When the case reached the Supreme Court, the brief prepared for the Jehovah's Witnesses objected that the "form of salute is very much like that of the Nazi regime in Germany."[92] Instead of respecting the value of religious freedom and individual conscience, Witnesses feared that their objection to the flag salute exposed them to persecution from groups who labeled them as unpatriotic. During the spring of 1940, with the German army moving across Europe, hundreds of attacks upon Jehovah's Witnesses in America from June 12 to June 20 were reported to the Justice Department.[93] On May 23, a mob in Del Rio, Texas, assaulted three Witnesses as supposed Nazi agents.[94] A June 2 Gallup poll reported

---

90. Id. at 586. See also Gobitis v. Minersville School Dist., 24 F.Supp. 271 (E.D. Pa. 1938).

91. Minersville School Dist. v. Gobitis, 108 F.2d 683, 692 (3d Cir. 1940).

92. Respondents' Brief, Minersville School Dist. v. Gobitis, at 3; 37 Landmark Briefs and Arguments of the Supreme Court of the United States: Constitutional Law 375 (Philip B. Kurland & Gerhard Casper, eds.).

93. Victor W. Rotnem & F. G. Folsom, Jr., "Recent Restrictions upon Religious Liberty," 36 Am. Pol. Sci. Rev. 1053, 1061 (1942).

94. Francis H. Heller, "A Turning Point for Religious Liberty," 29 Va. L. Rev. 440, 447 (1943).

that 65 percent of the public expected Germany to attack the United States.[95] Stores quickly sold out their supply of American flags.[96]

Given these conditions, would the Supreme Court protect individual liberties and religious freedom? The answer came on the last day of the Court's term, June 3, 1940. Writing for an 8–1 majority, Justice Frankfurter upheld the compulsory flag salute.[97] He began with this principle: "Certainly the affirmative pursuit of one's convictions about the ultimate mystery of the universe and man's relation to it is placed beyond the reach of law. Government may not interfere with organized or individual expression of belief or disbelief."[98] He proceeded to undermine that precise principle on the next page: "To affirm that the freedom to follow conscience has itself no limits in the life of a society would deny that very plurality of principles which, as a matter of history, underlies protection of religious toleration."[99] In short, individual conscience in this case would be subordinated to national needs.

Frankfurter explained that the Court's task, "as so often the case with courts, is to reconcile two rights in order to prevent either from destroying the other."[100] As his analysis unfolded, there was no reconciliation. The state had a right to destroy the religious rights of the Jehovah's Witnesses. He reached that conclusion by relying on a central premise: "National unity is the basis of national security."[101] From there

---

95. Id.

96. Id.

97. Minersville District v. Gobitis, 310 U.S. 586 (1940).

98. Id. at 593.

99. Id. at 594.

100. Id.

101. Id. at 595.

it was a short and easy step to conclude that forcing children to salute the flag, even if against their religious beliefs, helps foster national unity. He asserted: "The ultimate foundation of a free society is the binding tie of cohesive sentiment."[102] The "precise issue" to Frankfurter was whether state legislatures could adopt school policies that "evoke that unifying sentiment without which there can ultimately be no liberties, civil or religious."[103] Such a principle would find ready acceptance in Nazi Germany or any totalitarian state (see Box 5.3).

To Frankfurter, a compulsory flag salute was "surely" legitimate.[104] The wisdom of a compulsory flag salute "is

Box 5.3

Frankfurter's Argument for National Unity

Even if it were assumed that freedom of speech goes beyond the historic concept of full opportunity to utter and to disseminate views, however heretical or offensive to dominant opinion, and includes freedom from conveying what may be deemed an implied but rejected affirmation, the question remains whether school children, like the Gobitis children, must be excused from conduct required of all the other children in the promotion of national cohesion. We are dealing with an interest inferior to none in the hierarchy of legal values. National unity is the basis of national security. . . . The ultimate foundation of a free society is the binding tie of cohesive sentiment. . . . The precise issue . . . is whether the legislatures . . . of this country are barred from determining the appropriateness of various means to evoke that unifying sentiment without which there can ultimately be no liberties, civil or religious.

Source: Minersville District v. Gobitis, 310 U.S. 586, 595–97 (1940).

102. Id. at 596.
103. Id. at 597.

not for our independent judgment."[105] But of course it was. That is why the case was before the Court. To interfere with educational policy, Frankfurter said, "would in effect make us the school board for the country. That authority has not been given to this Court, nor should we assume it."[106] He therefore argued that the Court lacked jurisdiction. If so, why grant cert? He contradicted himself on the next page by citing a decision by the Court in 1925 that prohibited states from compelling all children to attend public schools.[107]

The remaining portions of his decision amounted to judicial double-talk: "The preciousness of the family relation, the authority and independence which give dignity to parenthood, indeed the enjoyment of all freedom, presuppose the kind of ordered society which is summarized by our flag."[108] Translation: the state may override family and parental values. The process of governmental control "may be utilized so long as men's right to believe as they please, to win others to their way of belief, and their right to assemble in their chosen places of worship for the devotional ceremonies of their faith, are all fully respected."[109] That does not follow. There is no respect for religious liberty if the state may compel children to salute the flag and violate their religious faith. Justice James Clark McReynolds, perhaps to distance himself from the reasons advanced by Frankfurter, concurred "in the result."[110]

---

104. Id. at 598.

105. Id.

106. Id.

107. Id. at 599; Pierce v. Society of Sisters, 268 U.S. 510 (1925).

108. Id. at 600.

109. Id.

110. Id. at 601.

In his dissent, Justice Harlan Fiske Stone rejected Frankfurter's emphasis on national security and national unity: "History teaches us that there have been but few infringements of personal liberty by the state which have not been justified, as they are here, in the name of righteousness and the public good, and few which have not been directed, as they are now, at politically helpless minorities."[111] He was not prepared to say that the right of the Gobitas children "to refrain from an expression obnoxious to their religion, is to be overborne by the interest of the state in maintaining discipline in the schools."[112]

The Jehovah's Witnesses, having prevailed in the lower courts, hoped the Supreme Court would protect their religious freedom. Instead, Frankfurter advised them to present their case "in the forum of public opinion and before legislative assemblies rather than to transfer such a contest to the judicial arena."[113] Stone objected that to defer to legislative judgment and the democratic process "seems to me no less than the surrender of the constitutional protection of the liberty of small minorities to the popular will."[114]

Despite the vigor of Stone's dissent, it had little impact on the other justices. He entered the conference room with the intent to defend the religious freedom of the Jehovah's Witnesses, but did not reveal his misgivings about Frankfurter's argument, nor did he circulate his dissent sufficiently early to attract votes to his side.[115] As relative newcomers to the

---

111. Id. at 604.

112. Id. at 606.

113. Id. at 600.

114. Id. at 606.

115. Alpheus Thomas Mason, Harlan Fiske Stone: Pillar of the Law 527–28 (1956). See also asterisked note on page 528.

Court, Hugo Black, William Douglas, and Frank Murphy deferred to Frankfurter because of his reputation as a civil libertarian. By the time they saw Stone's dissent, they decided it was too late to abandon Frankfurter.[116] Murphy's initial instinct was to write a dissent. He actually drafted one but did not circulate it.[117]

Far from accepting the Court's decision as the exclusive and final word on the meaning of the Constitution, Frankfurter's opinion was assailed by law journals, the press, and religious organizations. The *New Republic,* which Frankfurter helped found, warned that the country was "in great danger of adopting Hitler's philosophy in the effort to oppose Hitler's legions" and accused the Court of coming "dangerously close to being a victim of [war] hysteria."[118] A separate article tossed in some sarcasm: "Already Mr. Justice Frankfurter has been heroically saving America from a couple of school children whose devotion to Jehovah would have been compromised by a salute to the flag."[119] Out of thirty-nine law reviews that discussed *Gobitis,* thirty-one were critical, while newspapers condemned the Court for violating individual rights and buckling to popular prejudices.[120] Editorials in 171 newspapers tore apart Frankfurter's opinion.[121]

---

116. William O. Douglas, The Court Years, 1939–75, at 45 (1981).

117. J. Woodford Howard, Jr., Mr. Justice Murphy: A Political Biography 251 (1968); Peters, *supra* note 88, at 65–66.

118. "Frankfurter v. Stone," New Republic, June 24, 1940, at 843–44.

119. Walton Hamilton & George Braden, "The Supreme Court Today," New Republic, August 5, 1940, at 180.

120. David R. Manwaring, Render Unto Caesar: The Flag-Salute Controversy 158–60 (1962); Heller, *supra* note 94, at 452–53.

121. Mason, *supra* note 115, at 532.

Following release of the Court's decision, a wave of violence against Jehovah's Witnesses swept the country. By one estimate, the persecution of Witnesses from 1941 to 1943 marked the greatest outbreak of religious intolerance in twentieth-century America.[122] Stigmatized as disloyal, they became easy targets for arrests, forced marches, threats, beatings, vandalism, arson, and destruction of their buildings and property.[123] Justices Black, Douglas, and Murphy came to regret their decision to vote with Frankfurter without independently analyzing the constitutional issue. A few months after the decision, Douglas told Frankfurter that Black was having second thoughts about his vote. Sarcastically, Frankfurter asked whether Black had spent the summer reading the Constitution. "No," Douglas replied, "he has been reading the papers."[124]

Frankfurter's decision provoked such scorn and derision that it was not treated as a model worth emulating, even if it had the support of eight justices. Several state courts dismissed his opinion by offering greater protection to schoolchildren who cited religious reasons for not saluting the flag.[125] In 1942, Black, Douglas, and Murphy publicly announced that *Gobitis* was "wrongly decided,"[126] leaving Frankfurter with a shaky 5–4 majority. Chief Justice Charles Evans Hughes retired in 1941 and was succeeded by Stone. Two justices who had joined with Frankfurter (James F. Byrnes and Owen Roberts)

---

122. John T. Noonan, Jr., The Believer and the Powers That Are 251 (1987).

123. Peters, *supra* note 88, at 72–123.

124. H. N. Hirsch, The Enigma of Felix Frankfurter 152 (1981).

125. State v. Lefebvre, 20 A.2d 185 (N.H. 1941); In re Latrecchia, 26 A.2d 881 (N.J. 1942); State v. Smith, 127 P.2d 518 (Kans. 1942).

126. Jones v. Opelika, 316 U.S. 584, 624 (1942).

were replaced by Wiley Rutledge and Robert H. Jackson. Rutledge's opinions while on the D.C. Circuit suggested he would vote against Frankfurter.[127] If Jackson also voted to reverse *Gobitis,* Frankfurter would be left as a dissenter with two other justices.

By the time the flag-salute issue returned to the Court in the fall of 1942, the legal landscape had changed dramatically. A district court in West Virginia ruled that the state could not force the children of Jehovah's Witnesses to salute the flag. It did not feel bound by *Gobitis* because out of the seven justices now on the Court who participated in the 1940 decision, "four have given public expression to the opinion that it is unsound."[128] Justice Jackson, writing for a 6–3 majority, overruled *Gobitis* in 1943.[129] He prepared a masterful defense of individual freedom and religious liberty, but credit for the reversal belongs to those who refused to accept Frankfurter's opinion as the law of the land. Citizens around the country told the Court it did not understand the Constitution, minority rights, or religious liberty. Their independent voices prompted Black, Douglas, and Murphy to rethink their positions and switch sides.

Jackson's opinion, widely admired, has its limitations. Here is a passage frequently cited: "If there is any fixed star in our constitutional constellation, it is that no official, high or petty, can prescribe what shall be orthodox in politics, nationalism, religion, or other matters of opinion or force

---

127. E.g., Busey v. District of Columbia, 129 F.2d 24, 38 (D.C. Cir. 1942).

128. Barnette v. West Virginia State Board of Ed., 47 F.Supp. 151, 153 (D. W.Va. 1942).

129. West Virginia State Board of Education v. Barnette, 319 U.S. 624 (1943).

citizens to confess by word or act their faith therein. If there are any circumstances which permit an exception, they do not now occur to us."[130] The sentiment is generally sound, but often the Supreme Court attempts to decide what is orthodox. It releases a decision as though it presents the final and exclusive word on the Constitution. The ruling in *Gobitis* failed, as have many other decisions, including *Dred Scott, Plessy, Lochner,* the child-labor cases, and the trimester framework in *Roe* v. *Wade.* The true lesson from *Gobitis* is that no official—including those in the judiciary—may prescribe what is orthodox for the country.

Religious Liberty in the Military

In *Goldman* v. *Weinberger* (1986), a 5–4 Supreme Court decision upheld an Air Force regulation that prohibited an observant Jew in the military from wearing his yarmulke (skullcap) indoors while on duty. One year later, Congress passed legislation telling the military to rewrite the regulation to permit members of the military to wear religious apparel unless it interferes with military duties. How could the Supreme Court decide a constitutional issue involving individual rights and be reversed so quickly by Congress?

Captain Simcha Goldman, an Orthodox Jew and ordained rabbi, served for years in the U.S. Air Force as a psychologist in a mental health clinic. He wore his yarmulke on duty without incident. In April 1981, he testified at a court-martial on behalf of a defendant. A month later, in an apparent retaliatory move, the Air Force informed him that

---

130. Id. at 642.

wearing a yarmulke while on duty violated the military dress code.[131] His first remedy was to request that the Air Force permit an exception in his case. When the Air Force refused, the next step was a lawsuit.

A federal district court ruled that the Air Force regulation violated his religious freedom under the First Amendment.[132] The judge appeared to make light of the military's argument that allowing him to wear a yarmulke "will crush the spirit of uniformity, which in turn will weaken the will and fighting ability of the Air Force."[133] Another district court upheld the Air Force policy on yarmulkes, reasoning that departures from uniformity would adversely affect "the promotion of teamwork, counteract pride and motivation, and undermine discipline and morale, all to the detriment of the substantial compelling governmental interest of maintaining an efficient Air Force."[134] All three judges on a panel of the D.C. Circuit supported the Air Force position.[135] The Air Force argued that if it accommodated Goldman's yarmulke, other members of the military would offer their own religious claims: the use of turbans, robes, face and body paint, shorn hair, unshorn hair, badges, rings, amulets, bracelets, jodhpurs, and symbolic daggers.[136]

---

131. Goldman v. Weinberger, 475 U.S. 503, 511 (1986) (Stevens, J., concurring, joined by White, J., and Powell, J.).

132. Goldman v. Secretary of Defense, 530 F.Supp. 12 (D.D.C. 1981).

133. Id. at 16.

134. Bitterman v. Secretary of Defense, 553 F.Supp. 719, 725 (D.D.C. 1982).

135. Goldman v. Secretary of Defense, 734 F.2d 1531, 1535 (D.C. Cir. 1984).

136. Id. at 1539.

The D.C. Circuit voted against a motion to hear the case *en banc*. Three judges with quite familiar names dissented. One was Kenneth Starr, who later served as Solicitor General in the George H. W. Bush administration and as independent counsel during the investigation of President Bill Clinton. He said the panel's decision "does considerable violence to the bulwark of freedom guaranteed by the Free Exercise Clause."[137] The other two judges were Ruth Bader Ginsburg and Antonin Scalia, who would later move to the Supreme Court. In their view, the Air Force policy suggested "callous indifference" to Goldman's religious faith and ran counter to the American tradition of accommodating spiritual needs."[138]

Goldman took his case to the Supreme Court. A brief submitted by Solicitor General Charles Fried supported the Defense Department by arguing that if Goldman's position prevailed, it would force the military to choose between "virtual abandonment of its uniform regulations" and "constitutionally impermissible line drawing."[139] The entire purpose of uniform standards, he said, "would be defeated if individuals were allowed exceptions" and "make a mockery of the military's compelling interest in uniformity."[140] His reasoning was greatly exaggerated. Military regulations already allowed for "neat and conservative" religious apparel,

---

137. Goldman v. Secretary of Defense, 739 F.2d 657, 658 (D.C. Cir. 1984).

138. Id. at 660.

139. Brief for the Respondents, Goldman v. Weinberger, No. 84–1097, U.S. Supreme Court, October Term, 1985, at 19.

140. Id. at 49–50.

including the wearing of crosses, the Star of David, and various rings, bracelets, and other items of jewelry.[141]

During oral argument, Kathryn Oberly of the Justice Department advised the justices to leave the dispute to the elected branches: "If Congress thinks that further accommodation is either required or desirable it can legislate it."[142] Her suggestion was quite perceptive. The Court could not have the last word on this constitutional issue. Congress had full authority to trump the Court. Article I, Section 8, of the Constitution expressly provides that Congress shall "make Rules for the Government and Regulation of the land and naval Forces."

By the vote of 5 to 4, the Court held that the First Amendment did not prohibit the Air Force regulation. It accepted the Air Force judgment that the outfitting of military personnel in standardized uniforms "encourages the subordination of personal preferences and identities in favor of the overall group mission."[143] The Court's opinion was guided by the military values of uniformity, hierarchy, unity, discipline, and obedience to military effectiveness. A dissent by William J. Brennan, Jr. (joined by Marshall) offered conflicting arguments on which branch of government has the primary duty to protect individual rights. They faulted the Court for abdicating its role "as a principal expositor of the Constitution and protector of individual liberties in favor of credulous

---

141. Id. at 3–4.

142. Oral argument, Goldman v. Weinberger, U.S. Supreme Court, January 24, 1986, at 45.

143. Goldman v. Weinberger, 475 U.S. 503, 508 (1986).

144. Id. at 514.

deference to unsupported assertions of military necessity."[144] Yet they admitted that the elected branches also have a duty to protect religious freedom: "Guardianship of this precious liberty is not the exclusive domain of federal courts. It is the responsibility as well of the States and of the other branches of the Federal Government."[145] They urged Congress to fix the Court's mistake: "The Court and the military have refused these servicemen their constitutional rights; we must hope that Congress will correct this wrong."[146] Justices Harry Blackmun and Sandra Day O'Connor filed separate dissents.

Within two weeks of the decision, legislation was introduced in Congress to permit members of the armed forces to wear items of apparel not part of the official uniform. Members of the military could wear any "neat, conservative, and unobtrusive" item of apparel to satisfy the tenets of their religion. The Secretary of the military service could prohibit the wearing of an item after determining that it "significantly interferes with the performance of the member's military duties."[147] Various groups lobbied fiercely against the legislation: the American Legion, the Military Coalition, Secretary of Defense Caspar Weinberger, and the Joint Chiefs of Staff.[148] Nevertheless, the bill became law.[149] The Supreme Court balanced Goldman's religious liberty against military needs and came down on the side of the military. Congress engaged in the same kind of balancing exercise, but protected Goldman and religious liberty.

---

145. Id. at 523.

146. Id. at 524.

147. 132 Cong. Rec. 6655 (1986) (Senator Alfonse D'Amato); id. at 7042, 7211 (Senator Frank Lautenberg).

148. Louis Fisher, Religious Liberty in America 120–21 (2002).

149. 101 Stat. 1086–87, sec. 508 (1987).

The Supreme Court as Guardian of Individual Rights?

In 1937, President Franklin D. Roosevelt attempted to increase the size of the Supreme Court to enable him to control it through additional nominations. The Senate Judiciary Committee, controlled by Roosevelt's own Democratic Party, issued a vigorous repudiation of the court-packing plan. In doing so, it praised the Court as an essential guardian of individual and minority rights: "Minority political groups, no less than religious and racial groups, have never failed, when forced to appeal to the Supreme Court of the United States, to find in its opinions the reassurance and protection of their constitutional rights."[150] The record, of course, contains many failures.

Also in the late 1930s, Henry W. Edgerton (later a federal judge) was occupied in studying Supreme Court opinions from 1789 to the 1930s. His research concluded that judicial rulings offered little support for the theory that Congress had attacked, and the judiciary defended, individual liberties. Instead, federal courts regularly sided with the interests of government and corporations.[151] A few years later, in 1943, historian Henry Steele Commager offered a similar perspective. The Court had "intervened again and again to defeat congressional efforts to free slaves, guarantee civil rights to Negroes, to protect workingmen, outlaw child labor, assist hard-pressed farmers, and to democratize the tax system."[152]

---

150. S. Rept. No. 711, 75th Cong., 1st Sess. 20 (1937).

151. Henry W. Edgerton, "The Incidence of Judicial Control over Congress," 22 Corn. L. Q. 299 (1937).

152. Henry Steele Commager, Majority Rule and Minority Rights 55 (1943).

When I ask audiences to name a Supreme Court decision that upheld the rights of minorities, in almost every case they pick *Brown* v. *Board of Education* (1954). Certainly it was an important step forward to reject the "separate but equal" doctrine, but credit to the Court is qualified in many ways. First, the Court was striking down a doctrine it created. After almost six decades it finally announced: "We conclude that in the field of public education the doctrine of 'separate but equal' has no place. Separate educational facilities are inherently unequal."[153] Because the ruling was limited to public schools, the Court did not expressly overrule *Plessy*. Other decisions would be needed to strike down segregated facilities at beaches and bathhouses, golf courses, parks, community centers, buses, courtrooms, and bus terminal restaurants.[154]

Second, the principal force for political and legal change was not the Court. As political scientist John Denvir points out, *Plessy* "was overturned because a group of citizens refused to accept the Supreme Court's interpretation of the Fourteenth Amendment and engaged in a long, arduous, and ultimately successful struggle to have the Court correct its error."[155] Opponents of *Plessy* began by filing lawsuits not

---

153. Brown v. Board of Education, 347 U.S. 483, 495 (1954).

154. Beaches and bathhouses: Dawson v. Mayor, 220 F.2d 386 (4th Cir. 1955), aff'd, 350 U.S. 877 (1955); golf courses, parks, playgrounds, and community centers: Holmes v. City of Atlanta, 223 F.2d 93 (5th Cir. 1955), aff'd, 350 U.S. 879 (1955); Watson v. Memphis, 373 U.S. 526 (1963); buses: Browder v. Gayle, 142 F.Supp. 707 (M.D. Ala. 1956), aff'd, 352 U.S. 903 (1956) (explicitly overruling *Plessy*); courtrooms: Johnson v. Virginia, 373 U.S. 61 (1963); and bus terminal restaurants (interstate): Boynton v. Virginia, 364 U.S. 454 (1960).

155. John Denvir, Democracy's Constitution: Claiming the Privileges of American Citizenship 15–16 (2001).

against grade schools and high schools, but against segregated graduate schools and law schools.

In a 1936 case, black applicants had been denied admission to the law school at the University of Maryland. As compensation, the state offered to pay their tuition to a law school outside the state. A unanimous state appellate court in Maryland ruled that this policy violated the Equal Protection Clause. Blacks faced greater costs traveling to and living in another state. Moreover, education outside the state would not adequately prepare them for practicing in Maryland.[156] Similarly, Missouri wanted to give black students sufficient funds to cover their tuition costs at a law school in an adjacent state. The Supreme Court, divided 7 to 2, held the policy in violation of the Equal Protection Clause because it created a privilege for allowing white students to attend the Missouri law school while excluding blacks.[157] These decisions painted *Plessy* into an ever-narrowing corner.

The next effort in maintaining segregated education was to create a separate law school for blacks within Texas. A unanimous Court in 1950 concluded that the school for blacks did not satisfy the "separate but equal" doctrine. The University of Texas law school, attended by whites, was superior in terms of its professional staff, library, law review, moot court facilities, scholarship funds, distinguished alumni, tradition, and prestige.[158] Oklahoma tried a different tack. It agreed to admit blacks to the state university, but kept them

---

156. Pearson v. Murray, 182 A. 593 (Md. 1936).

157. Missouri ex rel. Gaines v. Canada, 305 U.S. 337 (1938). See also Sipuel v. Board of Regents, 332 U.S. 631 (1948) and Fisher v. Hurst, 333 U.S. 147 (1948).

158. Sweatt v. Painter, 339 U.S. 629 (1950).

separate from white students. Blacks had to sit in special seats in the classroom, and at special tables at the library and in the cafeteria. A unanimous Court in 1950 found this in violation of the Equal Protection Clause. The restrictions on a black student impaired the ability "to study, to engage in discussions and exchange views with other students, and, in general, to learn his profession."[159]

Third, quite beyond the Court's control were international developments. The horrors of racism in Nazi Germany, sending millions of Jews to their death in gas chambers and concentration camps, offered a chilling example of efforts to create a "master race." After the war, President Harry Truman took steps to desegregate the armed forces and confront racial discrimination within the federal government. The United States, emerging as a global leader after World War II, could not credibly fight world communism while practicing racial segregation at home. The federal government's *amicus* brief in *Brown* described the harmful effects of American segregation on U.S. foreign policy. Racial discrimination affected not only American blacks, but also dark-skinned visitors from other countries, providing "grist for the Communist propaganda mills."[160]

Fourth, the "unanimous" decision in *Brown* was highly misleading. In 1952 and through most of 1953, the Court was deeply divided on the constitutionality of segregated schools. Four justices (Black, Douglas, Burton, and Minton) were ready to overrule *Plessy*. Five (Vinson, Reed, Frankfurter,

---

159. McLaurin v. Oklahoma State Regents, 339 U.S. 637 (1950).

160. The government's brief was filed in December 1952; 49 Landmark Briefs 116–21. See Mary L. Dudziak, "Desegregation as a Cold War Imperative," 41 Stan. L. Rev. 61 (1988).

Jackson, and Clark) either supported *Plessy* or were loath to abandon it.[161] The death of Chief Justice Fred Vinson on September 8, 1953, and his replacement by Earl Warren seemed to produce a 5–4 majority to overrule *Plessy,* and Clark indicated he might shift to give the Court a 6–3 majority. Still, it was politically unattractive to have a divided Court reverse the 1896 decision.

Two of the Southerners on the Court (Tom C. Clark and Stanley Forman Reed) suggested they might join a unanimous decision if enforcement could be done in different ways, and at different times, by the states. Jackson and Frankfurter also supported flexibility. To attain unanimity, the Court decided to announce *Brown* in two steps: a broad ruling in 1954 to define constitutional rights (*Brown I*), followed by a second decision a year later to explain implementation (*Brown II*). The latter contained vague words and phrases, including the oxymoron "all deliberate speed."[162] Other phrases sent a green light to the states that they could take their time in desegregating public schools: "a practical flexibility," "as soon as practicable," "a prompt and reasonable start," with courts allowed to find that "additional time is necessary to carry out the ruling in an effective manner."[163] It is said that "justice delayed is justice denied." *Brown II* clearly announced that the road toward desegregating public schools would be lengthy with no clear deadline, inviting both procrastination and defiance.

---

161. S. Sidney Ulmer, "Earl Warren and the Brown Decision," 33 J. Pol. 688, 691–92 (1971); Richard Kluger, Simple Justice 589–614, 682–87, 696–99, 742–45 (1975); William O. Douglas, The Court Years, 1939–1975, at 113 (1980).

162. Brown v. Board of Education, 349 U.S. 294, 301 (1955).

163. Id. at 300.

Finally, *Brown I* awkwardly tried its hand at sociology: "Whatever may have been the extent of psychological knowledge at the time of *Plessy* v. *Ferguson,* this finding is amply supported by modern authority."[164] There followed a footnote to seven psychological and sociological studies on the effects of discrimination and segregation on children, raising questions about the Court's competence to distinguish between reliable and unreliable scholarship in this area.[165]

Weak implementation of *Brown II* resulted in little school desegregation. A decade later, the Court reflected on its language "all deliberate speed" by complaining: "There has been entirely too much deliberation and not enough speed."[166] A federal appeals court in 1966 announced it was a mistake to think the judiciary by itself could desegregate schools: "A national effort, bringing together Congress, the executive and the judiciary may be able to make meaningful the right of Negro children to equal educational opportunities. *The courts acting alone have failed.*"[167] The Civil Rights Act of 1964 made the difference. Congressional passage in the House (289–126) and Senate (73–26) sent a powerful signal to unite the public in support of minority rights. Legislative action—through extensive committee hearings and floor debate—and presidential speeches helped educate and persuade the country in a manner not possible by a Supreme Court decision.

---

164. Brown v. Board of Education, 347 U.S. at 494.

165. Abraham L. Davis, The United States Supreme Court and the Uses of Social Science Data 48–61, 95–118 (1973).

166. Griffin v. School Board, 377 U.S. 218, 229 (1964).

167. United States v. Jefferson County Board of Education, 372 F.2d 836, 847 (5th Cir. 1966) (emphasis in original).

Conclusion

A Broad and Continuing Dialogue

In a religious liberties case in 1997, the Supreme Court claimed to possess the last word on the meaning of the Constitution. It begins with this general perspective: "Our national experience teaches that the Constitution is preserved best when each part of the Government respects both the Constitution and the proper actions and determinations of the other branches." A fair and acceptable generalization. However, it then adds: "When the Court has interpreted the Constitution, it has acted within the province of the Judiciary Branch, which embraces the duty to say what the law is. *Marbury* v. *Madison,* 1 Cranch, at 177." The citation to *Marbury* is pointless and empty. Obviously it is also the duty of Congress and the president "to say what the law is." *Marbury* stands for many things, but it offers not the slightest support for judicial supremacy, nor did the case ever make that claim. The decision in 1997 concludes that when a conflict occurs between a Court precedent and a congressional statute, the Court's ruling "must control."[1]

Contrary to the Court's position, nothing in "our national experience" justifies the claim that when the Supreme Court

---

1. Boerne v. Flores, 521 U.S. 507, 535–36 (1997).

decides a constitutional issue, its ruling is final and binding on the elected branches. In the examples offered in this book, major Court rulings were more fluid than fixed, frequently overturned either by the Court or by statute and public opposition. Some decisions, such as *INS* v. *Chadha,* met with substantial noncompliance. In the yarmulke case of *Goldman* v. *Weinberger* (1986), the Court rejected Captain Goldman's plea for religious liberty. Within one year, Congress operated under its Article I authority over military regulations to pass legislation that protected the religious rights of members of the military.

Rulings by the Supreme Court are subject to challenges not only from the elected branches but also from the public at large. *Dred Scott,* in 1857, helped precipitate the Civil War and led to a constitutional amendment to nullify the Court's opinion.[2] *Plessy's* "separate but equal" doctrine in 1896 met increasing resistance from Americans, leading to lawsuits that chipped away at its foundation until federal courts from 1954 through 1963 rejected the doctrine.[3] The Court's "liberty of contract" theory in *Lochner* (1905) divided the judiciary and the nation until discarded in the late 1930s. Public opposition to the Court's flag-salute decision in 1940 helped convince three justices in the majority to shift their position within two years. The addition of two new justices produced an opinion in 1943 that reversed the earlier ruling.[4] The Court's trimester framework in *Roe* v. *Wade* (1973) encountered strong critiques from liberals and conservatives, resulting in a 1992

---

2. Dred Scott v. Sandford, 60 U.S. (19 How.) 393 (1857); discussed in Chapter Three.

3. Discussed in Chapter Five.

4. West Virginia State Board of Education v. Barnette, 319 U.S. 624 (1943), reversing Minersville School District v. Gobitis, 310 U.S. 586 (1940); discussed in Chapter Five.

decision that jettisoned this judicial overreach.[5] The Court's school busing decisions provoked such intense congressional and public opposition from 1971 into the early 1980s that the Court abandoned its policy.[6]

Respect for the judiciary does not mean blind deference and an unwillingness or incapacity of nonjudicial actors, including the public, to think independently and critically. Each branch needs informed, penetrating evaluations. From that level of scrutiny no branch should be immune. The aspiration for self-government and democracy cannot coexist with the doctrine of judicial supremacy.

No one doubts that Congress, like the Supreme Court and the president, can reach unconstitutional results. Justice William Brennan said in a 1983 dissent: "Legislators, influenced by the passions and exigencies of the moment, the pressure of constituents and colleagues, and the press of business, do not always pass sober constitutional judgment on every piece of legislation they enact."[7] It's a fair point, but the Supreme Court does not always pass sober constitutional judgment either. If we count the times that Congress has been "wrong" about the Constitution and compare those lapses with the occasions when the Court has erred, often by its own later admissions, the results make a compelling case for legislative confidence and judicial modesty.

Here are some observations to explain why the Supreme Court is not the last word on the meaning of the Constitution.

---

5. Planned Parenthood of Southeastern Pa. v. Casey, 505 U.S. 833 (1992), reversing the trimester framework in Roe v. Wade, 410 U.S. 113 (1973); discussed in Chapter Four.

6. Discussed in Chapter Four.

7. Marsh v. Chambers, 463 U.S. 783, 814 (1983) (Brennan, J., dissenting).

First, the fact that the Court upholds the constitutionality of a bill, as when it sustained the U.S. Bank in *McCulloch v. Maryland* (1819), places no obligation on the elected branches to agree with that judgment. Congress was later free to discontinue the bank. If it passed legislation to renew it, presidents (as Andrew Jackson did) were free to veto the bill on constitutional grounds. The elected branches were at liberty to exercise independent judgments. If they decided the bank had constitutional problems, they could abandon it. Over that decision the Court had no control. Similarly, the Supreme Court in 2012 upheld the Affordable Care Act, but no one should assume this ruling ends the constitutional debate. Congress and presidents will continue to rethink and most likely modify parts of the statute.

Second, a decision by the Court that a certain practice is not prohibited by the Constitution, such as the use of search warrants against a student newspaper in *Zurcher* v. *Stanford Daily* (1978), did not prevent the elected branches from passing legislation to abolish search warrants and adopt the less-intrusive subpoena power.[8] Rights unprotected by the courts may be secured by Congress, the president, and the states.

Third, when the Court concludes that an activity has no constitutional protection in federal courts—for example, distributing petitions in a shopping center, as in *PruneYard Shopping Center* v. *Robins* (1980)—states are not inhibited from protecting those actions by interpreting their own constitution.[9] Decisions by the Court may set a floor, or minimum, for constitutional rights. States may exceed those rights by acting through independent decisions under their constitutions.

---

8. 436 U.S. 547 (1978). For congressional action on the subpoena power, see Louis Fisher & Katy J. Harriger, American Constitutional Law 226-28 (10th ed., 2013).

9. 447 U.S. 74 (1980).

Fourth, the Court generally announces broad guidelines: "undue burden," "compelling governmental interest," "narrowly tailored," and "all deliberate speed." It is left to elected officials, jurors, and members of the public to apply those general principles to particular disputes, many of which will never reach the Supreme Court. The Court defines the edges. Nonjudicial actors fill in the vital and important middle. For example, the Court provides general guidance on what constitutes obscene materials (e.g., "prurient interest"). It is up to jurors to decide whether a book, movie, or photographic exhibit belongs in their community. The last word is there, not with the Supreme Court.

Fifth, through threshold doctrines (standing, ripeness, mootness, etc.), the Court often sidesteps a constitutional issue and leaves it to the regular political process. Article I, Section 9, of the Constitution requires that "a regular Statement and Account of the Receipts and Expenditures of all public Money shall be published from time to time." However, the Central Intelligence Agency and other agencies of the intelligence community received covert funding for decades. By invoking the standing doctrine, the Court refused to decide this constitutional question.[10] Years later, in 2007, Congress passed legislation to make public the aggregate budget of the intelligence community.[11] Many other constitutional issues have been settled outside the courts.[12]

Sixth, decisions by the Supreme Court are not pure creative acts, producing something out of nothing. They depend

---

10. United States v. Richardson, 418 U.S. 166 (1974).

11. Louis Fisher, Defending Congress and the Constitution 65–69 (2011).

12. Louis Fisher, "Separation of Powers: Interpretation Outside the Courts,"18 Pepp. L. Rev. 57 (1990); http://www.loufisher.org/docs/ci/460.pdf. Accessed Feb. 19, 2013.

on precedents and values established by other actors, both at the national and state levels. Long before *Gideon* v. *Wainwright* (1963), many states had decided that due process required that attorneys be appointed to represent indigent defendants.[13] The Supreme Court of Indiana in 1854 stated that "a civilized community" could not prosecute a poor person and withhold counsel.[14] In 1859, the Wisconsin Supreme Court called it a "mockery" to promise a pauper a fair trial and tell him he must employ his own counsel.[15] Congress in 1892 passed legislation to provide counsel to represent poor persons.[16] Not until 1963 did the Court announce its judgment.

Finally, states have substantial discretion under their constitutions to flatly disagree with the U.S. Supreme Court. In 1968, the Court held that a New York statute permitting textbooks to be "lent" free to students in grades seven through twelve, including children attending private and religious schools, was constitutional. The Court upheld the statute by concluding that the benefit extended to parents and children, not to the schools.[17] A number of states, looking to their constitutions that specifically prohibit the use of public funds to assist private and religious schools, rejected the child-benefit theory.[18]

In 1982, the U.S. Supreme Court collided with a state court but came out the loser. The Supreme Court of Washington in 1980 held that a university police officer had invalidly

---

13. Gideon v Wainwright, 372 U.S. 335 (1963).

14. Webb v. Baird, 6 Ind. 13 (1854).

15. Carpenter v. Dane, 9 Wis. 249 (1859).

16. 27 Stat. 252 (1892). Congress extended that provision in 1910; 36 Stat. 866.

17. Board of Education v. Allen, 392 U.S. 236 (1968).

18. Fisher & Harriger, *supra* note 8, at 600–03.

seized incriminating evidence in a student's dormitory room. It determined that the evidence had been obtained illegally and could not be admitted at trial.[19] The U.S. Supreme Court reversed. Relying on its "plain view" doctrine, it said the police officer was in a place he was entitled to be (in the hallway outside the student's room, with the door wide open) and could see drug paraphernalia. Therefore, the evidence could be introduced at trial.[20]

The case returned to the state court for "further proceedings not inconsistent with this opinion." Sounds like judicial supremacy for the U.S. Supreme Court. No. The Supreme Court of Washington rejected the "plain view" doctrine. No such doctrine existed in the state. Whereas its 1980 decision had cited several federal decisions, this time the Supreme Court of Washington based its reasoning "solely and exclusively on the constitution and laws of the state of Washington." It concluded it was right the first time and excluded the evidence.[21] Final word.

In her book *The Majesty of the Law,* Justice Sandra Day O'Connor offered conflicting positions on judicial finality. At times she described the judiciary as "the final arbiters of the constitutionality of all acts of government," even citing language in *Marbury* on the Court's authority "to say what the law is."[22] Elsewhere, however, she showed an appreciation

---

19. State v. Chrisman, 619 P.2d 971 (Wash. 1980).

20. Washington v. Chrisman, 455 U.S. 1, 6 (1982).

21. State v. Chrisman, 676 P.2d 419 (Wash. 1984). See Louis Fisher, "How the States Shape Constitutional Law," 15 State Legislatures 37 (August 1989).

22. Sandra Day O'Connor, The Majesty of the Law: Reflections of a Supreme Court Justice 243 (2003).

for the mix of judicial and nonjudicial forces that constantly shape the Constitution. She spoke of the "dynamic dialogue between the Court and the American public" and understood that no one could consider *Roe* v. *Wade* as settling "the issue for all time."[23] More generally, she said that a nation "that docilely and unthinkingly approved every Supreme Court decision as infallible and immutable would, I believe, have severely disappointed our founders."[24]

A judicial ruling is not fixed and binding for all time simply because it has been issued. It is controlling if sound in substance and reasoning. In 1849, a dissent by Chief Justice Roger Taney urged the Court to keep an open mind. In his view, an opinion by the Court "is always open to discussion when it is supposed to have been founded in error, and ... its judicial authority should hereafter depend altogether on the force of the reasoning by which it is supported."[25] Also in dissent, Justice Louis Brandeis observed in 1932: "The Court bows to the lessons of experience and the force of better reasoning, recognizing that the process of trial and error, so fruitful in the physical sciences, is appropriate also in the judicial function."[26] The Court, as a creature of the Constitution, is an experiment as well, to be judged on the basis of its performance and respect for self-government, not on some abstract theory of judicial finality.

---

23. Id. at 45.

24. Id. at 45. On the complex dialogue about abortion by all three branches and the states, see Neal Devins, Shaping Constitutional Values: Elected Government, the Supreme Court, and the Abortion Debate (1996).

25. Passenger Cases, 48 U.S. 283, 470 (1849).

26. Burnet v. Coronado Oil & Gas Co., 285 U.S. 393, 407–08 (1932).

INDEX OF CASES

INDEX OF SUBJECTS

ABOUT THE AUTHOR

Louis Fisher worked for the Library of Congress for four decades as senior specialist in separation of powers with the Congressional Research Service and as specialist in constitutional law with the Law Library before retiring in August 2010. During that period he worked closely with members of Congress and their staff. On more than fifty occasions he testified before congressional committees on a range of constitutional issues, including executive privilege, committee subpoenas, executive lobbying, presidential reorganization authority, legislative vetoes, item vetoes, pocket vetoes, the Gramm-Rudman-Hollings bill, recess appointments, war powers, the state secrets privilege, NSA surveillance, national security whistleblowing, covert spending, biennial budgeting, and the balanced budget amendment. In 1987 he served as research director of the House Iran-Contra Committee, writing major sections of the final report.

Fisher is the author of more than twenty books, including *American Constitutional Law* (with Katy J. Harriger, 10th ed., 2013); the full list of his books and more than 470 articles appears on his personal website: http://loufisher.org. It provides links to his publications and congressional testimony. He has received the Dartmouth Book Award, the Neustadt

Book Award, and two Louis Brownlow Book Awards. Upon his retirement, he became scholar in residence at the Constitution Project and adjunct professor at the William & Mary Law School. In 2011 the National Capital Area Political Science Association gave him the Walter Beach Pi Sigma Alpha Award "in recognition of public service as a political scientist." In 2012 he received the Hubert H. Humphrey Award from the American Political Science Association "in recognition of notable public service by an individual trained in political science."

Fisher received his doctorate in political science from The New School for Social Research in 1967 and has taught at Queens College, Georgetown University, American University, Catholic University, Johns Hopkins University, and the law schools of William & Mary and Catholic University. He has been invited to speak in Albania, Australia, Belgium, Bulgaria, Canada, China, the Czech Republic, Denmark, France, Germany, Great Britain, Greece, Israel, Japan, Macedonia, Malaysia, Mexico, the Netherlands, Oman, the Philippines, Poland, Romania, Russia, Slovenia, South Korea, Sweden, Taiwan, Ukraine, and the United Arab Emirates.